Y0-CAF-770

Social Issues
in Literature

Patriarchy in Sandra Cisneros's *The House on Mango Street*

Other Books in the Social Issues in Literature Series:

Social Issues
in Literature

Patriarchy in Sandra Cisneros's *The House on Mango Street*

Claudia Durst Johnson, Book Editor

GREENHAVEN PRESS
A part of Gale, Cengage Learning

Detroit • New York • San Francisco • New Haven, Conn • Waterville, Maine • London

Christine Nasso, *Publisher*
Elizabeth Des Chenes, *Managing Editor*

© 2010 Greenhaven Press, a part of Gale, Cengage Learning

Gale and Greenhaven Press are registered trademarks used herein under license.

For more information, contact:
Greenhaven Press
27500 Drake Rd.
Farmington Hills, MI 48331-3535
Or you can visit our Internet site at gale.cengage.com

ALL RIGHTS RESERVED.
No part of this work covered by the copyright herein may be reproduced, transmitted, stored, or used in any form or by any means graphic, electronic, or mechanical, including but not limited to photocopying, recording, scanning, digitizing, taping, Web distribution, information networks, or information storage and retrieval systems, except as permitted under Section 107 or 108 of the 1976 United States Copyright Act, without the prior written permission of the publisher.

For product information and technology assistance, contact us at

Gale Customer Support, 1-800-877-4253
For permission to use material from this text or product, submit all requests online at www.cengage.com/permissions

Further permissions questions can be emailed to permissionrequest@cengage.com

Articles in Greenhaven Press anthologies are often edited for length to meet page requirements. In addition, original titles of these works are changed to clearly present the main thesis and to explicitly indicate the author's opinion. Every effort is made to ensure that Greenhaven Press accurately reflects the original intent of the authors. Every effort has been made to trace the owners of copyrighted material.

Cover image by Ulf Andersen/Getty Images.

LIBRARY OF CONGRESS CATALOGING-IN-PUBLICATION DATA

Patriarchy in Sandra Cisneros's The house on Mango Street / Claudia Durst Johnson, book editor.
    p. cm. -- (Social issues in literature)
    Includes bibliographical references and index.
    ISBN 978-0-7377-4800-0 (hardcover) -- ISBN 978-0-7377-4801-7 (pbk.)
    1. Cisneros, Sandra. House on Mango Street. 2. Patriarchy. 3. Mexican Americans--Social life and customs. I. Johnson, Claudia Durst, 1938-
    PS3553.I78Z82 2010
    813'.54--dc22

                                      2009040552

Printed in the United States of America
1 2 3 4 5 6 7 14 13 12 11 10

Contents

Introduction

Sandra Cisneros's *The House on Mango Street* is told from the point of view of Esperanza, a Mexican American girl in Chicago. The novella is arranged in a series of vignettes about Esperanza's immediate surroundings and her Latino neighborhood, called a barrio. Esperanza provides the reader with a portrait of the characters who live around her and their relationships; the houses and rooms they inhabit; their language, clothes, traditions; and even their games. The prevailing theme in the novella is her growing awareness of what some critics have labeled her marginality; that is, the various ways in which she is outside circles of acceptance and power of various kinds, from the country at large to her little home. That marginality is influenced by varying levels of patriarchy. Her poverty and ethnicity clearly close her off from mainstream American society, and both are interwoven into the main aspect of powerlessness in her own community—gender.

The history of the debasement of women and their long struggle to receive basic rights finally afforded them the rights to vote, to own property, and to have a say in the fate of their minor children. The context pertinent to *The House on Mango Street*, in the decades before its publication, involves the process of consciousness raising—an effort to get men and women alike to know and feel the injustices and limitations inflicted by the accepted views of a woman's nature and her "proper" place. Although women had assumed the work of men during World War II, women who did not *have* to work when the men returned were again relegated to their "proper" roles as wives, helpmates, and mothers. Women who did have to work were restricted to a few jobs such as factory and farming work, secretarial work, and schoolteaching. A lowly view of women prevailed: mentally and psychologically they were considered weaker than men and, therefore, the men in their lives were expected to make decisions for them.

These cultural constructions left women powerless over their own destinies. In 1963 writer Betty Friedan identified what was called "the problem with no name"; that is, the feeling of frustration and lack of importance and fulfillment felt by so many housewives. The concept so accurately expressed what many women were feeling, and what many men recognized, that it became a turning point. By 1967 public awareness of women's limitations had led to women's liberation organizations. At an antiwar meeting in 1968, hundreds of women staged "The Burial of Traditional Womanhood" in Arlington National Cemetery. Others in 1968 protested the demeaning values apparent in beauty contests in which women presented themselves and were regarded by male viewers solely as sex objects. By the mid-1970s colleges throughout the country had initiated women's studies programs. And the National Organization for Women had filed thousands of lawsuits defending women in job discrimination cases. Women's groups also made public the unacceptability of sexual harassment. But even though the media, books, courses, and conferences have done much to educate the public, discrimination and harassment continue today.

The irony for Esperanza is that, despite women's progress in the mainstream United States, her own isolated Chicano community continued its church-supported, oppressive patriarchy. The related issues Esperanza faces in the novella consist of the following:

- the forced labor women encounter in their community
- the imprisonment of women and girls in their homes
- the distrust of women's morals
- the sexual abuse of and violence against women
- the view of females' insignificance

• the view of women solely as sex objects

The critical commentaries that follow delve into these gender issues from a variety of perspectives. The patriarchy's view of women as children of little value is the focus of some writers, who see this attitude as leading to confinement and slavery. Some critics study *The House on Mango Street* as a revision of the predominantly male coming-of-age book; unlike typical examples of the genre, Cisneros's work centers on the concerns of girls. Her work is also different from other Latino literature, which tends to present an uncritical view of the patriarchy and predetermined female roles. Also discussed here is the need for a woman's space—a significant room or a house—one that is not ruled by men. Yet among these negative pressures, Esperanza finds writing and a mission to help other barrio women, and these roles offer her a distinct identity that still includes a connection to her roots.

The last six readings in this volume make clear the continuing problems of gender discrimination throughout the world: the unjust attitudes toward marriage and divorce in Mexico, sexual harassment and discrimination in the workplace in the United States, and the repression of women in the Middle East and Asia.

Chronology

December 20, 1954
Sandra Cisneros is born in Chicago.

1959
Begins her education in a public school.

1954–1966
The Cisneros family moves many times within Chicago.

1966
The Cisneroses buy a house in a Puerto Rican neighborhood of Chicago.

1968
Cisneros enters Josephium Catholic High School.

1972
Begins an undergraduate program at Loyola University in Chicago.

1976
Is accepted into the master of fine arts program in creative writing at the University of Iowa.

1971–1981
Works as a counselor in a Latino Youth Alternative High School in Chicago.

1980
Completes her master's thesis.

1980–1981
Gets a job as an administrative assistant at Loyola University and publishes her first book of poems, *Bad Boys*.

1982–1983

A grant awarded by the National Endowment for the Arts (NEA) enables Cisneros to travel in Europe and serve as poet in residence at the Karolyi Foundation in Vence, France.

1984

Publishes the novella *The House on Mango Street* and becomes director of Guadalupe Cultural Center in San Antonio, Texas.

1985

Receives the Before Columbus American Book Award for *Mango Street* and a Dobie-Paisano Fellowship.

1987

Publishes her master's thesis, *My Wicked, Wicked Ways*, a book of poems; becomes a visiting professor at California State University at Chico and is awarded a second NEA grant.

1991

Publishes *Woman Hollering Creek* with Random House and receives the Lannan Literary Award and other commendations for that book.

1994

Publishes *Hairs/Pelitos*, a children's book, and *Loose Woman*, a book of poems.

1995

Receives a MacArthur Foundation Fellowship.

2002

Publishes her novel *Caramelo, or Puro Cuento* with Alfred A. Knopf; receives honorary doctorate from Loyola University of Chicago.

2009

Goes on book tour to celebrate the twenty-fifth anniversary edition of *The House on Mango Street*.

Social Issues in Literature

CHAPTER 1

Background on Sandra Cisneros

Growing Up in a Patriarchal System

Robin Ganz

Robin Ganz is a literary critic who has written biographical sketches of such noted Latino/a authors as Sandra Cisneros and Gary Soto.

In the following excerpt, Robin Ganz portrays Cisneros's lonely position in a patriarchal family. Ganz explains how Cisneros's father uprooted his family in Chicago on a regular basis to return to Mexico to spend time with his mother. The subsequent returns to Chicago required finding a new place for the family to live and a new school for the children to attend, which tended to isolate Cisneros from her neighbors and classmates. Cisneros was also isolated within her family. Cisneros's father used to boast that he had seven sons—including her among the males and never mentioning his one daughter. However, Cisneros's mother, though dependent on Cisneros's father and managing a large family, made sure that Cisneros had time free from household chores to do homework and to read, and reading both filled the empty spaces left by the regular family relocations and developed in Cisneros an internal narrator who chronicled the events of her daily life. It wasn't until Cisneros was eleven that her family moved to a permanent resisdence in a Puerto Rican neighborhood in Chicago's Humboldt Park. Some of Cisneros's earliest attempts at expressing herself were poems written at the age of ten. She wrote poetry again as a sophomore in high school, with the encouragement of a young female English teacher. A few years later, after taking a creative writing course in college and entering the University of Iowa's Writers' Workshop, Cisneros realized

Robin Ganz, "Sandra Cisneros: Border Crossings and Beyond. (Special Issue: Varieties of Ethnic Criticism)," *MELUS*, vol. 19, no. 1, Spring 1994, pp. 19(11). Copyright © MELUS: The Society for the Study of Multi-Ethnic Literature of the United States, 1994. Reproduced by permission.

that her childhood was very different from that of her fellow students, and she used her experiences in the Humboldt Park neighborhood to write The House on Mango Street *and show those differences.*

For readers and writers of Chicana literature, the 1980s signalled the emergence of voices of power and pain which many previous decades of racism, poverty and gender marginalization had suppressed. Breaking a silence that had run long and deep, writers such as Lorna Dee Cervantes, Denise Chavez, Gloria Anzaldua, Cherrie Moraga and Sandra Cisneros converted the unyielding forces of gender and ethnicity which had historically bound and muted them into sources of personal and stylistic strengths. Before the literary explosion of the '80s—excluded from both the mainstream and from ethnic centers of power—the Chicana had been an outsider twice over. Sandra Cisneros derived inspiration from her cultural specificity and found her voice in the dingy rooms of her house on Mango Street, on the cruel but comfortable streets of the barrio, and in the smooth and dangerous curves of borderland arroyos. In her work, she charts new literary territory, marking out a landscape that is familiar to many and unfamiliar to many more. And yet, resonating with genuineness, testifying to the ability of the human spirit to renew itself against all odds, Cisneros's voice carries across and beyond the barriers that often divide us.

Born the only sister into a family of six brothers, Sandra Cisneros "dreamed [her]self the sister in the 'Six Swans'" fairy tale. Cisneros elaborates: "She too was an only daughter in a family of six sons. The brothers had been changed into swans by an evil spell only the sister could break. Was it no coincidence my family name translated 'keeper of swans?'" Cisneros was born on December 20, 1954, "the year of Rosa Parks." A year and a half later, her mother gave birth to another girl child who died in infancy, leaving Cisneros the "odd number in a set of men." That her birthplace and family home is Chicago characterizes the convergence of rootlessness and love that has shaped her family history. Her great-grandfather, whose family "boasted railroads and wealth," played the piano for the Mexican president at his mansion in Mexico City. The fortune, lost at the gambling tables, was half-cloaked in secrecy by the time her father was born. Cisneros writes: "Our ancestors, it seems, were great gamblers ... but this is never mentioned out of politeness, although I have disinterred a few ... for the sake of poetry." Her paternal grandfather, a military man who "survived the Mexican Revolution with a limp and a pension," had put enough aside to send Cisneros's father, Alfredo Cisneros Del Moral, to college. She writes: "Since my father had a knack for numbers, he intended to pursue an accounting career. However, he was not very interested in his books that first year, and when he failed his classes, my father ran away to the United States rather than face my abuelito's anger."

Alfredo Cisneros Del Moral and Cisneros's "vagabond uncle" wandered the Eastern Seaboard and spent a "naive few weeks in the South," unsure about whether they belonged in the front or the back of its Jim Crow buses and eating eggs morning and night because it was "the only English word they knew." Planning to "cut across country and head to California, because they heard there were many Mexicans there, and New York was beginning to get too cold," the brothers decided to stop in Chicago for one day to see what it was like. On that Autumn day, a chance meeting with Cisneros's mother, Elvira Cordero Anguiano, was to change the course of Alfredo's life. One day became a month and then a lifetime as love caused dreams of California to fade when Alfredo, "who liked children and wanted a large family," married Elvira and set up housekeeping, for the time being at least, in a run-down house in one of Chicago's poorest neighborhoods.

Although Elvira Cordero's family history is "blurred and broken," rooted in a town in Guanajuato whose name Cisneros doesn't know, she recognizes that her "mother's family is simple and much more humble that that of [her] father's, but in many ways more admirable." Cisneros recounts that:

> My mother's father was a hard-working Indian man, big-boned and strong, with a face made of stone. His wife, my maternal grandmother, was pale and quiet. She, too, worked very hard—for her stepmother who, as my mother tells it, was very cruel to her. And when the whirlwind of the revolution arrived, the people of the small towns were victims to the violence of war from both sides. My grandmother said, after a while you could not tell who was a federalista and who a revolucionario, both stole your chickens and raped your women. My grandfather came to the United States during this time and found work in Chicago with the railroads. All his life he would work with his hands. He saved his money and sent for his wife and her cruel relatives, and that is how my mother's family came to be here, through the railroad money my grandfather earned.

Regretting having "thrown away his college education," and obliged to find a way to support his family, Alfredo learned upholstering from his uncle, tio Perico (Uncle Parrot). Cisneros relates that her "father inherited this trade as well as the nickname." Soon the Cisneros family began a compulsive circular migration between Chicago and Mexico City that became the dominating pattern of Sandra's childhood. The origin of Alfredo's obsessive need to uproot his family with almost seasonal regularity apparently lies in his relationship with his mother. Here, Cisneros describes her paternal grandmother:

> She was a hysterical woman, over-sentimental, spoiled. (Come to think of it, she was not unlike myself.) She had favorites. Her best baby was my father whom she held tight to. As a result, we returned like the tides, back and forth to Mexico City. Each time we returned to Chicago, we had to find a new place to live, a new school.

The loneliness that grew in Cisneros as a result of Alfredo's nostalgic southward journeys conjoined with other forces to shape her passion for literature and her desire to become a writer. Cisneros's feeling of aloneness intensified as the family established its own unique dynamics. In the following passage, she characterizes the alliances into which her siblings composed themselves within the frame of the family portrait:

> The six brothers soon paired themselves off. The oldest with the second-oldest, the brother beneath me with the one beneath him and the youngest two were twins, genetically as well as socially bound. These three sets of men had their own conspiracies and allegiances, leaving me odd-woman-out-forever.

Each time the family returned to "yet another Chicago flat, another Chicago neighborhood, another Catholic school," Alfredo would seek out the parish priest in order to get a tuition break and "complain or boast" that he had seven sons. In her narrative recollection "Only Daughter," Cisneros writes that he meant siete hijos, seven children, and that she is sure that he didn't "mean anything" by that mis-translation. Yet as she heard him describe his family in this way to the Sears Roebuck employee who sold them their washing machine, to the short-order cook who served up Alfredo's ham-and-eggs breakfast, and to anyone else who would listen, Cisneros "could feel [her]self being erased and would tug [her] father's sleeve and whisper: 'Not seven sons. Six! and one daughter.'"

While Alfredo's attitudes most influenced Cisneros's incipient awareness of her feminist identity, it was Elvira who guided her intellect. A high school drop-out who "read voraciously," and "quite superseded [Alfredo] in intelligence and social awareness," Cisneros's mother was never to fulfill her intellectual promise in any material way and, sadly "limited by the restrictions of her generation," was "to be dependent on him 'her whole life." It would be easy to understand a tale of Elvira's bitterness about her lost opportunities to express herself but, apparently, lamentation and regret were not in her nature. Elvira capitalized on her abilities by making Cisneros the benefactor of her intellectual and literary dreams and accomplishments. Although the Cisneros family "did not have any books in the house, [Elvira] saw to it that [Sandra] had [her] first library card even before [she] knew how to read."

Tracing her evolution as a lover of reading and creating poetry and prose in "Living as a Writer: Choice and Circumstance," Cisneros recounts that:

> Because of my mother, I spent my childhood afternoons in my room reading instead of in the kitchen. . . . I never had to change my little brothers' diapers, I never had to cook a meal alone, nor was I ever sent to do the laundry. Certainly I had my share of housework to do as we all did, but I don't recall it interfering with my homework or my reading habits.

About growing up without the burden of endless housework, Cisneros said at a Chicana Poetry Conference in Santa Fe, New Mexico in October, 1991, "I felt guilty, but not that guilty." Soon Cisneros was a prodigious reader. She writes: "Had my sister lived or had we stayed in one neighborhood long enough for a friendship to be established, I might not have needed to bury myself in books the way I did." Around the time of her early passage into the unimagined world that books opened up for her, Cisneros began to hear a voice in her head, a narrator who chronicled the routine events that made up her life:

> "I want you to go to the store and get me a loaf of bread and a gallon of milk. Bring back all the change and don't let them gyp you like they did last time." In my head my narrator would add: . . . *she said in a voice that was neither reproachful nor tender. Thus clutching the coins in her pocket, our hero was off under a sky so blue and a wind so sweet she wondered it didn't make her dizzy.* This is how I glamorized

Sandra Cisneros. Ulf Andersen/Getty Images.

my days living in the third-floor flats and shabby neighborhoods where the best friend I was always waiting for never materialized.

In 1966, when Cisneros was eleven, the family somehow borrowed enough for a down payment on its first home which she describes as "an ugly little house, bright red as if holding its breath." The Cisneroses's move into a permanent home ended their nomadic migration which had dominated Cisneros's early years. For Cisneros, the transition from the apartment on Roosevelt Road into the new house in a Puerto Rican neighborhood on the North Side called Humboldt Park also represented an important step in her development as a writer because, "it placed [her] in a neighborhood, a real one, with plenty of friends and neighbors that would evolve into the eccentric characters of *The House on Mango Street*."

Cisneros composed her first poems at the age of ten, but doesn't recall writing any more poetry until her sophomore year of high school when a "bright and vivacious young woman" came to her school to teach English. A poet herself, Cisneros's teacher introduced her to the work of contemporary poets and asked her students to write about the Viet Nam War. . . .

Cisneros . . . did not pick up her pen again until her junior year at Loyola University when she took a Creative Writing class. Under her teacher's tutelage she applied and was accepted into the University of Iowa's Writers' Workshop where she began to study with Donald Justice. Unfortunately, he left on sabbatical and Cisneros, feeling isolated from familiar surroundings and alienated from the workshop which "was East Coast pretentious and operated totally without mercy or kind words," floundered from one imitation to the next. Although Cisneros claims that the Iowa Writers' Workshop failed her, she experienced an epiphany there that she frequently designates as the moment her writing acquired a voice. What's more, in the moment of revelation in Iowa, the role which awaited her in the literary world suddenly became known to her.

It happened like this: Cisneros was enrolled in "a marvelous seminar that spring called 'Memory and the Imagination.'" The students were heatedly discussing a book from their reading list, *The Poetics of Space*, written by the French theorist, Gaston Bachelard. As her classmates debated "archetypes . . . shells, with the shell as house with the house of the imagination, the attics and stairways and cellars of childhood," Cisneros felt foreign from the others, alienated and dispossessed of some communal knowledge which they shared and which she felt she would never understand. Suddenly she was homeless, having no such house in her memory. As a child she had read of such houses in books and her parents had promised her such a house, but the best they could offer was the dilapidated bungalow in an impoverished inner-city neighborhood. Sitting in that classroom, her face grew hot and she asked herself, "What [do I] know? What could I know? My classmates were from the best schools in the country. They had been bred as fine hot-house flowers. I was a yellow weed among the city's cracks." In that moment she realized that she had something to write about that her classmates had not experienced and would probably never be able to articulate with the understanding that she possessed. Cisneros recounts that, "this is how *The House on Mango Street* was born, the child-voice that was to speak all my poems for many years."

After earning her MFA from the University of Iowa's Writers' Workshop in 1978, for the next three years Cisneros taught writing to (former) high school drop-outs at Chicago's Latino Youth Alternative High School. Since the publication of *The House on Mango Street* in 1984, she has taught creative writing as the writer in residence at many universities all over the country and given hundreds of readings. *My Wicked Wicked Ways*, a stunning collection of poems, was released in

1987 to enthusiastic reviews. Her most recent tour de force, a collection of prose pieces entitled *Woman Hollering Creek and Other Stories*, published by Random House in April, 1991, marks her transition from the relative obscurity of the small ethnic press into the mainstream of American literary culture and, in fact, into international prominence.

In an interesting cycle, the childhood loneliness that propelled her from the "real" world into the more pleasing worlds of reading and creating books has evolved into an adult solitude that is now indispensable to her work as a writer. In a 1990 interview with Pilar Rodriguez Aranda, Cisneros joked that her relatives had long since given up questioning her about when she's going to get married. She goes on to explain that, while they seem to have grudgingly accepted her decision not to marry, they still don't understand it.

> Now instead of asking: "When are you going to get married?" they're asking: "What happened in your childhood? Who hurt you? Who did this to you?" And they don't realize . . . "Look at your own marriage, tia, look at your marriage, mother, look at your marriage, abuela, look at your marriage, tio, papa," I've never seen a model of a happy marriage, or I've never seen a marriage that is as happy as my living alone, I've never seen it!

> I have some friends who are married and they seem to be happy, but I can't imagine myself in that kind of relationship. I really like my solitude. I don't like being lonely, but I'm not lonely. I need to be alone to work. I have very close friends and very close men in my life, but I don't want them in my house. That's the difference. . . . My writing is my child and I don't want anything to come between us. I like to know that if I come home very late from teaching—and teaching is exhausting, as exhausting as factory work, except I work more hours and get paid more—I don't want to come home to a husband. I want to come home to my books, and if I want to, I want to be alone to think. As a writer you need time to think, even if you're not writing. . . .

I wish we had little lights on our forehead like confessionals had. When someone was inside, the little light used to go red: "Ocupado." I want one like that: "Don't bother me, I'm thinking." Some men do respect. But people cannot read your mind and know that you are thinking even though you're not writing. . . . When I'm living with a man, he becomes my project. . . . I like my oneness, and I think that's the way I work best.

Sandra Cisneros's discovery of her poetic voice in Iowa was, up until that time, the single most important moment in her life as a writer and the result of that insight was both the personal accomplishment and critical success of *The House on Mango Street.*

Cisneros's Ethnic Past Plays a Major Role in Her Creative Works

Eduardo F. Elias

Eduardo F. Elias, of the University of Utah, is a recognized scholar in the field of Latin American studies. He has written for the Dictionary of Literary Biography *and the* Latin American Theatre Review.

In the following excerpt, Elias introduces Sandra Cisneros's The House on Mango Street, *about a young Chicano girl who dreams of writing. The work takes much from Cisneros's own youth in a run-down Puerto Rican neighborhood on the outskirts of Chicago, Elias notes. She was one of the first Chicano authors to receive training in a fine arts program, receiving her master of fine arts degree from the University of Iowa, one of the most prestigious writing programs in the nation. In realizing the differences between her background, attitude, and writing style and those of the mostly white, male students, Cisneros came to find her true voice. As she matured, Elias observes, she began taking a greater interest in the lives of Chicana women.*

Sandra Cisneros considers herself a poet and a short-story writer, although she has also authored articles, interviews, and book reviews concerning Chicano writers. She began writing at age ten, and she is one of the few Chicano authors trained in a formal creative-writing program. At the University of Iowa Writers' Workshop she earned a Master of Fine Arts degree in 1978. She has taught creative writing at all levels and has experience in educational and arts administration.

Eduardo F. Elias, "Sandra Cisneros," in *Dictionary of Literary Biography, Vol. 122, Chicano Writers. Second Series*, edited by Francisco A. Lomelí and Carl R. Shirley, Detroit, MI: Gale Research, 1992, pp. 77–81. Copyright © 1992 by Gale Research Inc. All rights reserved. Reproduced by permission of Gale, a part of Cengage Learning.

Her creative work, though not copious, has already been the subject of scholarly papers in the areas of Chicano and women's studies. . . .

Family Background

Cisneros is a native of Chicago, where she grew up and attended Loyola University, graduating in 1976 with a B.A. [bachelor of arts degree] in English. Her father was born in Mexico City to a family of means; his wanderlust and lack of interest in schooling led him to travel broadly and to venture into the United States. By chance he traveled through Chicago, met Sandra's mother, and decided to settle there for life. He and his family were influential in Sandra's maturation. Her mother came from a family whose men had worked on the railroad. Sandra grew up in a working-class family, as the only girl surrounded by six brothers. Money was always in short supply, and they moved from house to house, from one ghetto neighborhood to another. In 1966 her parents borrowed enough money for a down payment on a small, ugly, two-story bungalow in a Puerto Rican neighborhood on the north side of Chicago. This move placed her in a stable environment, providing her with plenty of friends and neighbors who served as inspirations for the eccentric characters in *The House on Mango Street*.

The constant moving during her childhood, the frequent forays to Mexico to see her father's family, the poor surroundings, and the frequent changing of schools made young Cisneros a shy, introverted child with few friends. Her love of books came from her mother, who saw to it that the young poet had her first library card before she even knew how to read. It took her years to realize that some people actually purchased their books instead of borrowing them from the library. As a child she escaped into her readings and even viewed her life as a story in which she was the main character manipulated by a romantic narrator. . . .

Cisneros's Differences Shape Her Voice

Cisneros looks back on those years and admits she did not know she was a Chicana writer at the time, and if someone had labeled her thus, she would have denied it. She did not see herself as different from the rest of the dominant culture. Her identity was Mexican, or perhaps Puerto Rican, because of the neighborhood she grew up in, but she mostly felt American—because all her reading was of mainstream literature, and she always wrote in English. Spanish was the private language of home, and she spoke it only with her father. Cisneros knew no Chicano writers in Chicago, and although she was the only Hispanic majoring in English at Loyola, she was unaware of being different—in spite of her appearance, which was considered exotic by her female classmates. . . .

The bulk of Cisneros's early writing emerged in 1977 and 1978. She began writing a series of autobiographical sketches influenced by Vladimir Nabokov's memoirs. She purposely delighted in being iconoclastic, in adopting themes, styles, and verbal patterns directly opposed to those used by her classmates. *The House on Mango Street* was born this way, with a child's narrative voice that was to be Cisneros's poetic persona for several years.

The poem "Roosevelt Road," written in the summer of 1977, is most important to Cisneros because it forced her to confront the poverty and embarrassment she had lived with all her previous years and to admit the distinctiveness of this background as a positive resource that could nourish her writing. In this poem the language is completely straightforward and descriptive of the tenement housing where the poet lived as a child. Lines run into one another, so that the reader is compelled to follow the inherent rhythm, while working on the sense of the message:

We lived on the third floor always

because noise travelled down

The milkman climbed up tired everyday

with milk and eggs

and sometimes sour cream.

Mama said don't play in alleys

because that's where dogs get rabies and

bad girls babies

Drunks carried knives

but if you asked

they'd give you money.

How one time we found that dollar

and a dead mouse in the stone wall

where the morning glories climbed. . . .

Dedicated to the Women

By the time that *The House on Mango Street* was ready for publication, Cisneros had out-grown the voice of the child narrator who recounts the tales in the book, but this 1983 work gave Cisneros her broadest exposure. It is dedicated to "the women," and, in forty-four short narratives, it recounts the experiences of a maturing adolescent girl discovering life around her in a Hispanic urban ghetto. There are many touching scenes that Esperanza, the young narrator, recounts: her experiences with the death of relatives and neighbors, for example, and with girlfriends who tell her about life. In "Hips," young Esperanza explains: "The bones just one day open. One day you might decide to have kids, and then where are you going to put them?" Esperanza identifies herself to her readers: "In English my name means hope. In Spanish it means too many letters." As the stories of Esperanza in her Hispanic barrio evolve, the child breezes through more and more maturing experiences.

The reader sees many portraits of colorful neighbors—Puerto Rican youths, fat ladies who do not speak English, childhood playmates—until finally Esperanza sees herself and her surrounding experiences with greater maturity. Thus the reader sees her at her first dance in the tale "Chanclas," where attention is first focused on the bulky, awkward saddle oxfords of a schoolgirl, then the vision is directed upward as Esperanza blossoms into a graceful and poised dancer, who draws everyone's glances. Esperanza retells humorous experiences about her first job and her eighth-grade girlfriend who marries; then Esperanza reveals more of her intimate self in the last two tales. In "A House of My Own" and "Mango Says Goodbye Sometimes," it is revealed that the adolescent has been nurturing a desire to flee the sordid, tragicomic environment where she has grown up. The image of the house is also useful to reveal the need for the narrator to find a self-identity.

A Feminine View

An important contribution by Cisneros to Chicano letters is that this book about growing up offers a feminine view of the process, in contrast to that exemplified by leading works by men. As critics Erlinda Gonzales-Berry and Tey Diana Rebolledo have aptly pointed out, young Esperanza is a courageous character who must combat the socialization process imposed on females; the character breaks from the tradition of the usual protagonist of the female bildungsroman [the coming of age genre] by consistently rejecting the models presented to her and seeking another way to be Chicana: "I have begun my own kind of war. Simple. Sure. I am one who leaves the table like a man, without putting back the chair or picking up the plate." Esperanza's experiences parallel those depicted by other Chicana writers.

In conversations about her life, Cisneros admits that up through her college years she had always felt that she was not her own person. Thus Esperanza yearns for "a house all my own. . . . Only a house quiet as snow, a space for myself to go, clean as paper before the poem." Cisneros's speaker feels the need to tell the world the stories about the girl who did not want to belong to that ugly house on Mango Street. Esperanza admits, at the conclusion of her stories, she is already too strong to be tied down by the house; she will leave and go far, only to come back some day for those stories and people that could not get away. The conclusion is that, in essence, Cisneros takes within her the memories from the house as she also carries her mementos from Mango Street, her bag of books and possessions. These are her roots, her inspirations, and the kernels of what Cisneros sensed, years ago in Iowa, that distinguished her from other American writers.

An Advocate for Unheard Chicana Women

Michelle M. Tokarczyk

Michelle M. Tokarczyk is a poet and a professor of English at Goucher College in Baltimore, Maryland. Her books include For a Living: Poetry at Work.

According to Tokarczyk, growing up in a society that believed women's only proper vocation was to be wives and mothers caused Sandra Cisneros to treasure her independence and to vow to speak for the voiceless—that is, the women in her culture to whom her book is dedicated. Tokarczyk's excerpt details how the blend of cultures in Cisneros's community was fraught with complications of racism, poverty, and sexism. Leaving home and securing an apartment of her own in Chicago was, for a Chicana woman, an unbelievable accomplishment—one that made her exhilarated and proud. The turbulent sixties brought change to Cisneros, Tokarczyk notes, as women and minorities began breaking out of their stereotypes. She adds that Cisneros's class consciousness and ethnic awareness grew along with her feminism.

Much of Cisneros's work . . . can be classified as Latina bildungsroman [coming-of-age genre], for it depicts protagonists' efforts to come of age within their communities and families, and it speaks for more than the protagonist. Cisneros has said that one of her goals is to give voice to the voiceless, to represent the lives of Chicanas, working-class Mexican-American women. Indeed, Cisneros is credited with opening doors for Latina writers through both her linguistic

Michelle M. Tokarczyk, "The Voice of the Voiceless: Sandra Cisneros," in *Class Definitions: On the Lives and Writings of Maxine Hong Kingston, Sandra Cisneros, and Dorothy Allison*, Selinsgrove, PA: Susquehana University Press, 2008, pp. 96–145. Copyright © 2008 by Rosemont Publishing & Printing Corp. All rights reserved. Reproduced by permission.

experimentation and her celebratory treatment of women. She has created a new, hybrid voice, one that is bicultural and bilingual, one that reflects her experiences and surroundings. Her writing is both realistic and childlike and engaging. It reflects the rhythms of working-class Mexican and Mexican-American lives, especially the lives of women grappling with racism, cultural issues, and patriarchy. As reviewer Patricia Hart says, Cisneros portrays women who struggle to make something beautiful out of the ugliness fate has dealt them. . . .

Cisneros's Early Background

Sandra Cisneros's beginnings were in an economically insecure, but loving working-class family. She was born in 1954 in a poor Latino/Latina neighborhood in Chicago that was composed primarily of Puerto-Rican Americans, but also included Chicanas and Chicanos. Her family moved frequently, often to areas that, according to Cisneros, resembled photos of European cities after World War II: neighborhoods filled with empty lots and burned-out buildings. Since her father was a favored offspring, the family regularly went to Cisneros's paternal grandparents' home in Mexico City. These visits provided a semblance of stability in their peripatetic lives and, as importantly, gave the children a truly bicultural, binational heritage. Cisneros has said she feels lucky to have a truly close relationship with Mexico that many Chicanos and Chicanas lack. Eventually, Chicago life stabilized. By the time she was twelve, the Cisneros family had bought a house of their own. It was this house, viewed through Cisneros's adult eyes, that became the inspiration for Esperanza's home in *The House on Mango Street.*

Although both of Cisneros's parents were of Mexican ancestry, their class backgrounds were considerably different, a fact that likely sensitized Cisneros to class difference. . . .

Cisneros's own mother was undoubtedly a major influence on her. In an interview with Dorothy Allison, Cisneros says she could not have been a writer if her mother had been a more traditional woman. Despite having borne eight children, Cisneros's mother is described by the author as a "very male woman," an anti-Catholic who is very bright. (Indeed, she made sure all her children had library cards as soon as they were eligible for them.)...

An Outsider from the Start

Sandra Cisneros was the third surviving child and only daughter in a family that included six sons. (A girl born after Cisneros died young.) In this male-dominated, traditional Mexican-American household, conduct and behavior were strictly defined according to culturally prescribed gender parameters....

Being the only daughter was often an isolating experience, for Cisneros had no sisters with whom to play or share her thoughts. The family's constant moving, which often involved changing schools, made it difficult for her to develop friendships. Furthermore, she was painfully shy. Because she was too timid to raise her hand in class or volunteer to answer questions, her grades suffered. Moreover, like many poor immigrant families, hers tried hard to minimize expenses. She had only one school uniform. Her mother accidentally burned it while ironing and then patched it rather than buy another. Wearing this mended clothing made Cisneros feel "raggedy," inevitably undercutting her self-confidence. Sadly, Cisneros recalls, "I was the girl with the C's and D's. I was the ugly kid in the class with the bad haircut." As a result, she spent considerable time alone, reading and daydreaming....

Through her reading, Cisneros educated herself. She reflects negatively on her years at Catholic schools where the education was rudimentary, the nuns often insensitive, and the students often biased against Latinas. Throughout middle school and high school, she wrote stories; and in high school, she served as editor of the school literary magazine, but did not come to think of herself as a "serious" writer until her undergraduate years. She chose Loyola University because a brother went there. Her generation was the first in her extended family to attend college; in part, Cisneros's father agreed to send his daughter there because he thought she'd get her "MRS" degree: find a husband. Undoubtedly, it was also less threatening to have his daughter commute to college from their home than to send her away. So even though Cisneros had a grant that would have covered her dormitory costs, she remained at home during her undergraduate years, as do many first-generation working-class students. Overall, she found the education adequate, but not challenging. As she reflects back on her experience, however, she says that Divine Providence put her where she needed to be. Loyola University finally hired a creative writer to teach some classes. Rather than find a spouse, Cisneros found her talent.

While she was in college, Cisneros had her first boyfriend. Undergraduate romances often dissolve, and this one did, too, in part because her boyfriend was too traditional, too possessive, and too intrusive on her private time. Moreover, she did not want to be like good, respectable women she knew who were trapped in relationships with possessive men. . . .

An Independent but Lonely Life

For many years, Cisneros was often angry with Mexican men, not for their treatment of her per se, but for their attitude toward Chicanas in general. Some of her reactions are common for women of color. For example, Cisneros was frequently disturbed to see Mexican men with white women, feeling that such relationships suggest these men don't love themselves or their mothers. Yet perhaps because getting involved with a Mexican man might have been more likely to lead to marriage, Cisneros was, like the prototypical *femme macho*, especially guarded with her feelings around them.

In her interview with Dorothy Allison, she tells of how restricted she felt as a Latina, and how she could not achieve her goals and be a wife and mother—at least not early in her career. Yet it was incredibly difficult for a Latina to live a life without children and a husband. When she was still living in Chicago, [Chicana-literature critic and feminist] Norma Alarcón visited her, and after quickly scanning the apartment and finding no children's toys or man's clothing, asked, "You live by yourself?" "Yeah." "How did you do it?" "When she said that," Cisneros recalls, "that is when my feminism began, right there, because I felt like crying. Because I did not realize how hard it had been to arrive at that apartment of my own and no one had understood how hard it was for me until Norma asked." Working-class ethnic women did not leave home for careers—even white working-class women rarely did so. At this point, Cisneros understood that not everyone cried every weekend; she did because the choice she made, although absolutely necessary and ultimately rewarding, was nonetheless profoundly lonely and alienating. Repeatedly, she has emphasized her lack of role models, a situation typical of working-class writers, particularly woman writers. To this day, she lacks these models, but she has more faith in her own choices and more experience in making choices. After her graduation from Loyola, she began an uncharted path toward becoming a writer. In the coming years, she would represent girls and women who were making a similar journey.

Still Marginalized in Graduate School

In 1976, Cisneros was accepted into the University of Iowa's prestigious creative writing program in poetry and for the first time moved away from a Latina/Latino environment. Given the school's reputation, she undoubtedly had high expectations. Indeed, she studied with such distinguished poets as Louise Gluck, William Anderson, Bill Matthews, Donald Justice, and Marvin Bell. Unfortunately, graduate school was no more positive for Cisneros than her undergraduate years were. A fellow student who has become a friend, Dennis Mathis, described the program as a pressure cooker. Students had to compete for financial aid of various amounts and prestige. (Cisneros received none.) Furthermore, students in the writing workshops criticized with brutal honesty that verged on cruelty. More importantly, the mid 1970s were the last years of the old boy era at the university. The spirit of the program, according to Mathis, is captured by 1960s photos hanging up. "The students sitting around the table were all male, guys with skinny ties and suits, horn-rimmed glasses, cigarettes. You could just tell they all wanted to be the next James Jones or John O'Hara or [Ernest] Hemingway. You know—tough guy stories about their army years, affairs with older women, fishing." Needless to say, these pictures included no working-class women of color. . . .

Feminist and Ethnic Context

Fortunately, many social changes in the turbulent 1960s facilitated Cisneros's acceptance as a writer with a unique voice. Although Mexican-Americans have always had a strong ethnic and racial identity, in the 1960s they became increasingly politicized. One of the most obvious signs of this politicalizaton is the adaptation of the term *Chicana*, a name derived from the word *Mexicano/Mexicana*. The word *Chicana* itself is a politically rich one, embracing the Mexican identity in what [Mexican American feminist and writer] Gloria Anzaldúa calls "*la raza*," the *mestiza* race that evolved when Spaniards and Native Americans intermingled. It also carries connotations of the Mexican laboring, working-class identity; hence, the term shocked some upwardly mobile and middle-class Mexican-Americans. According to Norma Alarcón, the appropriation of the term *Chicano/Chicana* by Mexican-Americans during this period was part of the demand for an ethnic history that "became a call for the recovery and rearticulation of the record to include the stories of race/class relations of the silenced against whom the very notions of being Mexican or not Mexican, being American or not American, and being a citizen or not a citizen had been constructed." The word *Chicana* is thus a rich one capturing the intersections of race, class, and gender.

An integral part of the emerging Chicana consciousness is a Chicana feminism that, like mainstream American feminism, developed out of grassroots political movements rather than intellectual centers in universities. Chicana feminism, however, as [Chicana poet and writer] Cherrie Moraga points out, borrowed minimally from white feminism; if there was any borrowing, it was perhaps from black feminists. . . . One of the most influential Chicana critics and activists was Gloria Anzaldúa, who theorized the notion of a *mestiza* consciousness that acknowledges the overlapping, sometimes conflicting identities of indigenous person, Spaniard, and mixed race or *mestiza*. In *Borderlands/La Frontera* Anzaldúa sees the United States/Mexico border over which many Mexicans and Mexican-Americans regularly cross as a metaphor for a life on the hyphen in which multiple identities are constantly balanced and shifted. . . . As [literary scholar] Timothy Libretti argues, a Chicana perspective on class reasserts and complicates a Marxist one, for it is comprehensive, including race, gender, and culture as class determinants. Chicana feminists "indict a Marxism that theorizes class as a pure and primary category, ignoring that the uneven experiences of class conditions one's race and gender, that race and gender condition one's class positioning, and that a first world's working class might be complicit with the exploitation and oppression of a colonized or internally colonized third world working class." In this respect, Chicana feminism resembles black feminism expressed in the work of critics such as Patricia Hill Collins and the Black Feminist Statement of 1977. It might be described as womanist because it reflects the standpoint of minority women and exhibits class awareness. . . .

As her class and ethnic consciousness deepened, Cisneros began to realize she was not alone as a writer. In the 1970s, a literature that would better reflect Cisneros's experiences was emerging. Poetry was first the dominant genre: one thinks of the work of Victor Cruz and the Chicano Renaissance poets or, in the 1980s, Miguel Algarin and the Nuyorican Poets Café. These poets, unlike some contemporary academic ones, valued the oral tradition, often singing or reciting their words to their communities. It took women somewhat longer to gain the necessary education and identify themselves as writers.

Social Issues in Literature

CHAPTER 2

Patriarchy in *The House on Mango Street*

Cisneros Revises the Traditional Coming-of-Age Story

Leslie S. Gutiérrez-Jones

Leslie S. Gutiérrez-Jones is a lecturer in English at the University of California, Santa Barbara.

In the following excerpt, Gutiérrez-Jones explores the form of The House on Mango Street as a new kind of bildungsroman, or growing-up novel, bringing up a variety of topics with regard to gender. She contrasts the predominant coming-of-age genre, clearly a masculine form, with Esperanza's story: In the male literary territory, a young boy rebels and escapes from his oppressive family, society, and church as he focuses starkly on himself— his independence and his individualism. Sandra Cisneros "poaches" this form but turns it into a girl's story of awakening and awareness—not only of herself but of the people, especially the women, around her. Gutiérrez-Jones concludes that counter to the male hero, Esperanza looks out, not in, with sympathy.

Just as Esperanza must leave behind her dependence on rented spaces and on standards external to her own experience, so Cisneros, a Chicana writer, is faced with the challenge of creating a home in the midst of a predominantly white, predominantly male, literary tradition: that of the *Bildungsroman* [coming-of-age novel]. Writer and character both face the conflict between desire for self-expression and fear of being co-opted by the very forms of self-expression available. The individual focus of writing, and particularly of the genre

Leslie S. Gutiérrez-Jones, "Different Voices: The Re-*Bildung* of the Barrio in Sandra Cisneros' *The House on Mango Street*," in *Anxious Power: Reading, Writing, and Ambivalence in Narrative by Women*, edited by Carol J. Singley and Susan Elizabeth Sweeney, Albany, NY: State University of New York Press, 1993, pp. 295–312. Copyright © 1993 State University of New York. Reproduced by permission of the State University of New York Press.

of the Bildungsroman, threatens to betray that aspect of identity which most calls out for expression: membership in a community. Only a fierce loyalty to this connection provides an adequate response, for Esperanza as for Cisneros, to the ambivalences generated by individual artistic achievement. Like her protagonist, who insists that the house of her own *cannot* be "a man's house"—especially "not a daddy's"—Cisneros must insistently remake the conventions and formulas of a patriarchal individualistic tradition, using them in order to transform them, tactically appropriating them in order to make them her own . . . and, by extension, her community's.

A Woman's Genre

One model for understanding what is at stake in such an appropriation may be found in [critic] Michel de Certeau's analysis of the creative art forms of the disempowered, the "subtle, stubborn, resistant activity of groups, which, since they lack their own space, have to get along in a network of already established forces and relationships." For the marginalized writer, the "already established forces and relationships" are represented by the literary tradition of the dominant culture. . . . Cisneros, in de Certeau's terms, "poaches" upon the supposedly private reserve of the white male Anglo-European literary tradition, moving like a nomad "across fields she did not write." Like Esperanza, she can neither purchase nor inherit a "ready-made" structure to call home, but instead creates from within a new space, a home in the heart where her fellow transients are welcome. . . .

When [critic] Esther Labovitz tackles the problematic issue of defining a female Bildungsroman, she astutely identifies a number of the changes such a hybrid would entail, especially concerning distinctions between male and female parameters of rebellion; yet she assumes that the female Bildungsroman evolved naturally during the twentieth century in response to women's improved social conditions, developing belatedly as "cultural and social structures appeared to support women's struggle for independence." . . .

Cisneros' narrator does finally achieve a sense of calm resolution, but it is not the resolution of surrender or acceptance; rather, Esperanza insists with quiet determination that she has "gone away to come back." She has left behind her selfish desire to escape, alone, from the barrio of Mango Street, not to return "until somebody makes it better." Realizing "Who's going to do it? The mayor?" Esperanza commits herself to changing, not accepting, the established order—to becoming that somebody who is emphatically not the mayor and who will indeed try to make it better. Esperanza's final determination to return to Mango Street "for the ones [she] left behind. For the ones who cannot [get] out" reflects a crucial point of difference from the sacred ground of the literary genre upon which Cisneros is poaching. . . .

Coming to Terms Rather Than Leaving

As narrator, Esperanza creates and chronicles her developing identity not through self-absorbed introspection, but by noting, recording, and responding to the lives around her—those lives for whom almost half of the collection's forty-four "prose poems" are named, and whose significance is underscored by Cisneros' title, which situates Esperanza not as a solitary loner but as she comes to perceive herself: a product and member of a particular community. Immune to the "privilege of power" associated with glorifying the individual, Esperanza comes to understand that the three strange sisters, and her friend Alicia, are right: Mango may say "goodbye *sometimes,*" but even when set free from the physical locale, Esperanza "will *always* be Mango Street" (my emphases). Protagonists like Cisneros' might be outsiders vis à vis the dominant culture, yet they are emphatically not loners. Unlike the traditional "American" hero, who underscores his independence by

The House on Mango Street *tells the coming-of-age story of Esperanza, a Mexican American girl who learns life lessons as part of an involved community. She looks forward to leaving the barrio of Mango Street to realize her potential, but she also wants to return there to make a difference.* Image copyright © Andresr, 2009. Used under license from Shutterstock.com.

isolating himself on the high seas (Captain Ahab), in the wilderness (Thoreau), in the "territories" (Huck Finn), or on the road (Jack Kerouac), Cisneros' hero has no such choice. Esperanza has already been symbolically cast out of mainstream "American" suburbia; her status as outsider is not chosen, but imposed. Yet she does not react to her exteriority by perceiving herself as "alone against the world." Rather, Esperanza defines herself as a member of a community—the community that is Mango Street. . . .

Cisneros' Esperanza explores the difficulties—and the possibilities—inherent in the struggle for . . . a balance, as she learns that neither self nor community can sustain itself independently; each requires the other. For example, when she senses the difficulty of reconciling "femininity" with conventional notions of adulthood, she determines "not to grow up tame like the others" and instead practices her "own quiet war," "leav[ing] the table *like a man*, without putting back the chair or picking up the plate" (emphasis mine). But this strategy of male emulation only shifts the burden to her mother (whose sacrifices are described in the segment which immediately follows), and casts herself into the role of the "bad" woman, the villainess in the movies "with red red lips who is beautiful and cruel." Esperanza admires the selfishness of this woman whose "power is her own. She will not give it away," yet when she tries to envision such an identity for herself, the callousness of such power brings her to an abrupt—and disturbing—realization. . . .

Responsibility to Community

Esperanza . . . realizes the implications of her talents, acknowledging in her final vignette that she will indeed go far: "one day I will say goodbye to Mango. I am too strong for her to keep me here forever." And yet her power and freedom are both circumscribed and expanded through being shared. She will never be like the "tame" women "who lay their necks on the threshold waiting for the ball and chain"; but neither will she be like Stephen Dedalus [the protagonist in James Joyce's *Portrait of an Artist as a Young Man*], who sees his art as a function of his own autonomy, necessitating his abandonment of home, fatherland, and church. Esperanza senses her ongoing responsibility: not toward the centers of (relative) power, the fathers and husbands who contribute to the oppression of Mango Street's women by demanding obedience and docility, but toward those to whom Cisneros has dedicated the work: "*A las Mujeres*" [to the women]. Her loyalty is toward the less powerful, the less strong, the less articulate in the dominant language: toward those, the sisters remind her, "who cannot leave as easily as you." . . .

No Life in Isolation

Esperanza does not learn lessons [of acceptance and compassion] as an isolate individual, but rather shares them (as do the weird sisters), as part of a group: as one of three girlhood friends, in the case of mocking Lupe, or as part of a general "we" of Mango Street, in the case of "Those Who Don't." Her budding feminism, like this sensitivity to the dynamics of exclusion, is also gained through interaction and involvement with others. She recognizes the dangers of her gender and refuses the threatened "ball and chain" partly in response to the experiences and warnings of others (for example, her mother in "A Smart Cookie") and partly in response to her own experiences with harassment and abuse, the majority of which either occur in the company of her friends ("The Family of Little Feet"), or result from a betrayal by more "sophisticated" classmates like Sally ("The Monkey Garden" and "Red Clowns"). . . . Esperanza does not experience—or narrate— the harsh lessons of growing up as an autonomous, self-absorbed individual, but as a sensitive and involved member of a community. . . .

By determinedly marching away, yet with equal determination promising a return and reconciliation, Esperanza achieves a sense of balance between her own needs and the needs of her community—to the benefit of both. . . .

The House on Mango Street, then, despite its apparently "single" narrator, expresses the multiplicity of focus found in many recent works of fiction by women: Alice Munro's *The Lives of Girls and Women*, Gloria Naylor's *The Women of Brewster Place*, Joan Chase's *During the Reign of the Queen of Persia*, Louise Erdrich's *Love Medicine*, Nicholasa Mohr's *Rituals of Survival*, Alison Lurie's *Only Children*, and Amy Tan's *The Joy Luck Club*. Telling a communal story diffuses the problematic ideology of individualism, and allows female writers the opportunity to explore (and potentially to resolve) tensions between group involvement and individual autonomy—tensions that cannot be addressed within a literary tradition glorifying a single protagonist. The genre of the Bildungsroman, then, provides a particularly treacherous, yet particularly rewarding, ground for Cisneros' "poaching." As the young Esperanza must create an identity for herself in a fictional world which denies selfhood to members of her sex, her class, and her ethnic group, Cisneros must create her own space, and assert her own voice, within a culture not historically open to her; her tactic of poaching upon the Bildungsroman provides an opportunity, as it were, to renovate and remodel the rented cultural space of this patriarchal genre, in order to make it her own.

A New Cultural Myth Empowers Women

Reuben Sánchez

Reuben Sánchez is professor of English at California State University at Fresno. His specialties are children's literature and the works of John Milton.

In the following excerpt, Sánchez approaches The House on Mango Street *through cultural myths, which shape and explain the worldview of a particular community. It is his argument that Sandra Cisneros rejects the male-centered, Catholic myth of her Chicano culture. She produces a new myth based on her own experiences. Through the eyes of a child, Cisneros contrasts true home versus homelessness in the barrio, rejecting the traditional home's patriarchal misuse and imprisonment of women. Esperanza's attachment to the women's fate is the main thread running through the young girl's story, Sánchez asserts, and it is a clue to the reason she must first run away and then return for the women, either physically or symbolically through literature. In Sánchez's view, the reason Esperanza must leave is because she is determined not to submit to the patriarchal myth that would oppress her.*

Through story telling the writer's perception of the world is manifested. We might think of myth, therefore, as cultural story telling, a way by which the writer who belongs to and identifies with a particular community explains why the world is the way it is, from the point of view of that particular community. The writer either validates a myth, or modifies a myth without rejecting it, or rejects a myth and creates a new myth

Reuben Sánchez, "Remembering Always to Come Back: The Child's Wished-For Escape and the Adult's Self-Empowered Return in Sandra Cisneros's *House on Mango Street*," *Children's Literature*, vol. 23, 1995, pp. 222–38. Copyright © 1995 The Johns Hopkins University Press. Reproduced by permission.

based on his or her own experience. In *The House on Mango Street*, Sandra Cisneros participates in the third type of story telling by combining myth (home) and irony (homelessness) in her depiction of life in the barrio as seen through the eyes of a girl.

Home Versus Homelessness

Cisneros addresses the theme of home versus homelessness in a series of forty-four vignettes—some as short as a few paragraphs, others as long as four or five pages—written in a language that is easily accessible and in a style that is sophisticated in its presentation of voice and theme. There is no single narrative strand, though the vignettes are loosely connected to each other in that they concern a brief period in which Esperanza, the book's protagonist, lives on Mango Street. We are never told her age, but she seems to be about ten or eleven years old. She wishes to find a house of her own:

> Not a flat. Not an apartment in back. Not a man's house. Not a daddy's. A house all my own. With my porch and my pillow, my pretty purple petunias. My books and my stories. My two shoes waiting beside the bed. Nobody to shake a stick at. Nobody's garbage to pick up after.
>
> Only a house quiet as snow, a space for myself to go, clean as paper before the poem.

This type of story telling incorporates both extremes—home contrasted with homelessness, the ideal house contrasted with the realistic, harsh surroundings—into a larger myth concerning the child's perception of her world and her rejection of the patriarchal myth that would prevent her from finding a house of her own. To free her protagonist of one myth, Cisneros must create another myth.

Esperanza recognizes the reality of her own homelessness, for she points out that until they move into the house on Mango Street her family has lived in several different houses;

on Mango Street she continues to wish for her ideal house, a wish that initiates and concludes the narrative, the narrative thus ending with a type of return, a tradition in children's literature. There is closure to the narrative in the repetition of a specific passage at the end of *The House on Mango Street*. At the beginning Esperanza states, "We didn't always live on Mango Street. Before that we lived on Loomis on the third floor, and before that we lived on Keeler. Before Keeler it was Paulina, and before that I can't remember. But what I remember most is moving a lot." Near the end she reiterates, "We didn't always live on Mango Street. Before that we lived on Loomis on the third floor, and before that we lived on Keeler. Before Keeler it was Paulina, but what I remember most is Mango Street, sad red house, the house I belong but do not belong to." What Esperanza adds to the second passage evinces her discovery that although what she remembers *initially* is moving often, what she remembers *finally* is Mango Street. The addition to the second passage suggests that there has been a change in Esperanza from the beginning to the end of her story telling, where her concern is with a particular neighborhood and a particular house, to which she vows she will return. . . .

The Patriarchal Myth

Powerlessness is no longer a condition experienced primarily by women, children and other oppressed people. It is a condition we all recognize." Powerlessness is of course Esperanza's condition, and she is in danger of remaining powerless. Showing why the female is powerless enables Cisneros to offer a way by which her protagonist may empower herself. Esperanza learns that she can empower herself through "books and paper"—a form of "deceit" in that books and paper enable her to "subvert" the "physical, economic and linguistic traps in women's and children's literature." . . .

The Chicana's concern with "place"—a house, or a room of one's own—is a reaction against the patriarchal myth that denies the Chicana a place of her own. Whereas the Chicano is free to journey through the mountains or the cities, the Chicana's movement has often been restricted by the Chicana writers themselves. The reality the Chicana addresses, then, is the reality of her restriction to the urban setting—particularly the house or the room. That setting is Esperanza's past and her present in *The House on Mango Street*; she recognizes that it might well be her future as well. . . .

The Lost Garden

Cisneros addresses the home versus homelessness theme in an urban rather than pastoral setting. In the vignette "The Monkey Garden," she shows why the pastoral must be rejected—a rejection, certainly, of the pastoral image of Eden, perhaps a postlapsarian [after the Fall] vision of Eden, for this garden is overgrown *and* decaying. The urban world has overtaken the pastoral world in that the garden becomes a junk yard where "Dead cars appeared overnight like mushrooms." In the garden, too, Esperanza, brick in hand, realizes that Sally does not want to be "saved" from "Tito's buddies." This realization results in a form of self-expulsion in that Esperanza now feels she no longer belongs in the garden: "I looked at my feet in their white socks and ugly round shoes. They seemed far away. They didn't seem to be my feet anymore. And the garden that had been such a good place to play didn't seem mine either." It is time, she senses, for her to leave the garden and what it represents. She is changing, outgrowing that which kept her in the garden until now, and she expresses that awareness through a reference to her feet and shoes—one of many references to feet and shoes in Cisneros's book. Others may be found, for example, in "The Family of Little Feet" and "Chanclas" (a *chancla* is a type of slipper or old shoe), vignettes concerned with the confusion involved in the transition from childhood to adolescence.

Cisneros presents the image of the garden in order to reject it. Any attempt to return to an edenic past would be ironic for the female who seeks freedom from the patriarchal Genesis myth. Though Esperanza may not fully understand why, she nonetheless feels that she no longer belongs in the garden: "Who was it that said I was getting too old to play the games?" Nor does she require a deity to evict her. The theme of exile from the garden—the recognition and rejection of what the garden represents—is specifically related to the home versus homelessness theme: the home Cisneros rejects is the patriarchal, edenic home. . . .

In the vignette "Beautiful & Cruel," Esperanza declares that she will rebel against the traditional role expected of her by acting like a man: "I have begun my own quiet war. Simple. Sure. I am one who leaves the table like a man, without putting back the chair or picking up the plate." Yet, only three vignettes later in "Red Clowns," which immediately follows "The Monkey Garden," Esperanza becomes a victim. She goes with Sally to the carnival, where Sally goes off with a boy and leaves Esperanza alone. What happens next is not clear, but it appears that Esperanza is raped, or if she is not, the experience is just as traumatic. . . .

Rejecting the Old Myths

Esperanza will diverge from that pattern, we assume, for only two vignettes after "Red Clowns" Esperanza meets las comadres in the vignette "The Three Sisters." Esperanza will destroy the male myth, not by literally destroying the garden as Nina does, but by becoming a writer and writing about her past.

Cisneros's critique of patriarchal society—the forms of power through which it protects its "fraternal cause"—and her reaction against that society are evident through much of the book. . . . Esperanza seeks to possess this kind of power. In the vignette "My Name" she declares that "the Chinese, like the Mexicans, don't like their women strong." Although she has inherited her grandmother's name, Esperanza will not "inherit her place by the window." Instead, she will "baptize" herself "something like Zeze the X," a name whose very sound conjures resistance, a cacophonous name that she feels will help her assert her power to avoid her grandmother's fate. Esperanza decides "not to grow up tame like the others who lay their necks on the threshold waiting for the ball and chain." Vowing to break away from what confines her makes Esperanza "dangerous" (a word Cisneros uses often in the book): "Them are dangerous," Mr. Benny points out to Esperanza and her friends. "You girls too young to be wearing shoes like that. Take them shoes off before I call the cops, but we just run." . . . Sally, too, is considered dangerous because of the type of clothes and shoes she wears, as Esperanza says to her: "I like your black coat and those shoes you wear, where did you get them? My mother says to wear black so young is dangerous, but I want to buy shoes just like yours, like your black ones made out of suede, just like those." Esperanza is fascinated by what is deemed dangerous. . . .

References to Children's Literature

In certain instances in *The House on Mango Street*, the references to children's literature also serve as metonyms through which Cisneros develops the home versus homelessness theme and the rejection of the patriarchal myth theme. For example, in the vignette "Edna's Ruthie," Esperanza tells how she had memorized "The Walrus and the Carpenter" from [Lewis Carroll's] *Through the Looking-Glass*, and one day recited it to Ruthie, a friend, "because I wanted Ruthie to hear me." In Tweedledee's poem the unsuspecting oysters are tricked and then eaten by the walrus and the carpenter. Esperanza's selection of this story is not accidental, as it bears special relevance to her vow not to be overpowered by the society in which she lives—her vow, that is, "not to grow up tame like the others who lay their necks on the threshold waiting for the ball and chain."

Besides the Alice [in Wonderland] books, there is another text that Cisneros uses in her characterization of Ruthie. Esperanza describes Ruthie's whistling as "beautiful like the Emperor's nightingale." This fairy tale serves as a metonym of the world in which Ruthie and Esperanza live. In [Hans Christian] Andersen's "The Nightingale," the emperor, one of the last people in his realm to know about the nightingale, finally recognizes and appreciates the beauty of its song. He cages the nightingale, however, so that it can sing only for the court. An artificial nightingale is later manufactured and brought to the court, which results in the loss of interest in the live nightingale; no one notices when the nightingale escapes back to the forest. But when the artificial nightingale breaks and the music is gone, the emperor begins to grow weak. With Death sitting on his chest and the demons of his past surrounding the emperor, the nightingale returns from the forest and rescues him through the beauty of its song. The nightingale then agrees to come and sing for him from time to time, though the emperor must promise not to tell anyone.

According to Esperanza—who perhaps got it from Ruthie herself—Ruthie was married and left Mango Street only to be forced to return and live with her mother:

> She had lots of job offers when she was young, but she never took them. She got married instead and moved away to a pretty house outside the city. Only thing I can't understand is why Ruthie is living on Mango Street if she doesn't have to, why is she sleeping on a couch in her mother's living room when she has a real house all her own, but she says she's just visiting and next weekend her husband's going to take her home. But the weekends come and go and Ruthie stays.

Of course, Ruthie does not have "a real house all her own," and that is Cisneros's point. Like Andersen's nightingale, Ruthie is caged and ignored. For example, if she was indeed married, then she is ignored by her husband. Nor does her mother seem to show much affection for her: "Once some friends of Edna's came to visit and asked Ruthie if she wanted to go with them to play bingo. The car motor was running, and Ruthie stood on the steps wondering whether to go. Should I go, Ma? she asked the grey shadow behind the second-floor screen. I don't care, says the screen, go if you want. Ruthie looked at the ground. What do you think, Ma? Do what you want, how should I know? Ruthie looked at the ground some more. The car with the motor running waited fifteen minutes and then they left." The image of Ruthie is of a female literally trapped and unable to escape Mango Street, to escape "her mother's living room," for that matter. Ruthie is only one of many symbols in *The House on Mango Street* of the trapped female.

Esperanza Refuses to Be Trapped

For Esperanza, there is something at once sad and beautiful about Ruthie. Like Andersen's nightingale, Ruth is much admired and loved because she is undemanding and unselfish. She "sees" beauty and, for Esperanza, she possesses beauty: "Ruthie sees lovely things everywhere. . . . When we brought out the deck of cards that night, we let Ruthie deal. . . . We are glad because she is our friend." Interpreting the allusions to stories by Dodgson [Lewis Carroll's real name] and Andersen enables us to understand the themes Cisneros addresses through the characterization of Ruthie: the homelessness and the victimization of the female.

Ruthie loves books and says she "used to write children's books once," although now she seems unable to read, which suggests the possibility of losing the empowerment that comes through reading and writing. Books and paper give Esperanza the power to be dangerous and (possibly) to avoid Ruthie's fate. She recognizes that through the power of books and paper she will make the prophecies of the old woman (la comadre) and of the young woman (Alicia) come true:

One day I will pack my bags of books and paper. One day I will say goodbye to Mango. I am too strong for her to keep me here forever. One day I will go away.

Friends and neighbors will say, What happened to that Esperanza? Where did she go with all those books and paper? Why did she march so far away?

They will not know I have gone away to come back. For the ones I left behind. For the ones who cannot out.

She says that she will leave and that she will come back. But these actions are beyond the confines of the narrative—a narrative fragment, that is, to be resolved by the reader.

Perhaps most important, the power Esperanza acquires through books and paper will give her the strength to return. . . .

A New Myth for the Women

Mango Street is a place where Esperanza may have at times felt joy and a sense of belonging, but it is also a place where she realizes that women are locked in their rooms by jealous and insecure husbands, a world in which there is violence, incest, and rape. She describes a harsh world from which she seeks escape, but a world to which she must return empowered as writer.

At the end of *The House on Mango Street* Esperanza recognizes, and Cisneros validates, the empowerment that comes through writing and remembering. Hence, the writer can find her freedom, can find her voice as writer, though she can only find that freedom and voice by honoring an injunction: You *will* come back, she is told. She may or may not go far away, but she will come back for herself and "for the others." Here, then, is yet another circle in the book that includes those outside the fictional narrative, those to whom the book is dedicated, and those who will read the book, thereby perpetuating the circular journey of the child/adult each time the text is read. There is indeed a circle that binds, that extends beyond the confines of the narrative to bind las mujeres. Dedicating her book "A las Mujeres / To the Women," *Cisneros* has come back "For the ones who cannot out." The book's dedication and the very last line of the book form a circle symbolic of remembering always to come back.

A Rejection of Role Models That Lead to Oppression

Leslie Petty

Leslie Petty earned a PhD from the University of Georgia, specializing in feminist activism in American fiction written circa the beginning of the twentieth century.

In the following excerpt, Petty discusses the archetypes of the good woman (la Virgen de Guadalupe) and the bad woman (la Malinche) in Mexican culture and how they are represented in Sandra Cisneros's The House on Mango Street. *Petty argues that Cisneros shows the suffering and subjugation of the Virgin model in the person of her mother and her aunt, among others. The hardships of these people cause Cisneros to move away from the Virgin model toward the model of Malinche, who is represented by Marin and to some extent by Sally. However, the total rejection or betrayal of one's community that is part of the model of Malinche is rejected by Cisneros's protagonist, Esperanza, who determines not only to leave the barrio and become successful but also to come back and make the barrio a better place. Petty concludes that the characters of the Virgin and Malinche are fused in Esperanza, who shows how a Hispanic woman can transcend the limitations associated with each role model.*

In "And Some More," a story from Sandra Cisneros's *The House on Mango Street*, two young girls discuss the nature of snow:

> There ain't thirty different kinds of snow, Lucy said. There are two kinds. The clean kind and the dirty kind, clean and

Leslie Petty, "The 'Dual'-ing Images of la Malinche and la Virgen de Guadalupe in Cisneros's *The House on Mango Street*," *MELUS*, vol. 25, no. 2, Summer 2000, pp. 119–32. Copyright © MELUS: The Society for the Study of Multi-Ethnic Literature of the United States, 2000. Reproduced by permission.

dirty. Only two. There are a million zillion kinds, says Nenny. No two exactly alike. Only how do you remember which one is which?

At first glance, the girls' conversation appears to be a bit of childish nonsense, and, on a surface level, it is. Read in a broader context, however, Nenny and Lucy's debate highlights a conflict that is at the heart of Cisneros's work: the insistence on culturally defining the world by a rigid set of black/white, good/bad, clean/dirty dualities, versus the reality of individuality, uniqueness, and infinite differentiation. Cisneros comments on the difficulties inherent in this clear-cut dichotomy, and she relates this binary specifically to the Mexican influences in her life and writing:

Certainly that black-white issue, good-bad, it's very prevalent in my work and in other Latinas. We're raised with a Mexican culture that has two role models: La Malinche y la Virgen de Guadalupe. And you know that's a hard route to go, one or the other, there's no in-betweens.

According to Cisneros, then, females, like the snow, are not seen in Latino culture as unique individuals but are labeled as either "good" women or "bad" women, as "clean" or "dirty," as "virgins" or "malinches."

Cisneros is not the first writer to acknowledge the difficulties in dealing with this duality nor the cultural archetypes upon which it is based. As [literary scholar] Luis Leal observes, "the characterization of women throughout Mexican literature has been profoundly influenced by two archetypes present in the Mexican psyche: that of the woman who has kept her virginity and that of the one who has lost it." These archetypes, embodied in the stories of la Malinche, the violated woman, and la Virgen de Guadalupe, the holy Mother, sharply define female roles in Mexican culture based on physical sexuality; however, as historical and mythical figures, these two archetypes take on both political and social significance that also influence perceptions of femininity in the Latin American world.

As the Mexican manifestation of the Virgin Mary, la Virgen de Guadalupe is the religious icon around which Mexican Catholicism centers. Consequently, versions of her historic origin are prevalent throughout the national literature. Although several variations of the story of the Virgin's initial apparitions exist, [historian] Stafford Poole identifies the version published in 1649 by the Vicar of Guadalupe, a priest named Luis Laso de la Vega, as the definitive source. According to Poole's translation of de la Vega, la Virgen de Guadalupe originally appeared to a converted Indian, Juan Diego, in 1531, on the hill of Tepeyac, identifying herself as "mother of the great true deity God." The Virgin tells Juan Diego that she "ardently wish[es] and greatly desire[s] that they build my temple for me here, where I will reveal . . . all my love, my compassion, my aid, and my protection." Diego immediately proceeds to the bishop in Mexico City, but he is greeted with disbelief. On his second visit, the bishop asks Diego for proof of the apparition. The Virgin sends Diego to the top of the hill, where he gathers "every kind of precious Spanish flower," despite the fact that these flowers are out of season and do not grow on that hill, and the Virgin places them in his cloak. When Diego visits the bishop, the bishop's servants try to take some of the blossoms, but they turn into painted flowers. Finally, when Diego sees the bishop and opens his cloak, the flowers fall out, and an imprint of the Virgin is left on the lining of the cloak. The bishop becomes a believer, begs for forgiveness, and erects the shrine to la Virgen de Guadalupe on the hill of Tepeyac.

Several elements of this story are important in the development of the cult of la Virgen de Guadalupe that spread rapidly in Mexico after this apparition. As [renowned Mexican poet] Octavio Paz observes, "The Virgin is the consolation of the poor, the shield of the weak, the help of the oppressed. In sum, she is the Mother of orphans." In addition to her religious importance, Paz and others recognize the political significance of this nurturing aspect of the Virgin in the formation of a Mexican national identity. First, in *Quetzalcoatl and Guadalupe*, Jacques Lafaye makes the case that la Virgen de Guadalupe is a Christian transformation of Tonantzin, the pagan goddess who was originally worshipped on the hill of Tepeyac. This link with Aztec culture is important because it distinguishes the Mexican symbol from its Spanish counterpart, la Virgen de Guadalupe de Estremadura. Therefore, as Leal notes, la Virgen de Guadalupe de Tepeyac is "an Indian symbol," and she is "identified with what is truly Mexican as opposed to what is foreign." She is the "protector of the indigenous." Appropriately, the image of the Virgin was used on banners promoting independence during the Mexican Revolution, and today she is revered as the "Queen of Hispanidad," giving la Virgen de Guadalupe a political designation in Latin American tradition in addition to her religious significance. . . .

The antithesis of the pure maternal image of la Virgen de Guadalupe in [what Paz calls] the Mexican "dual representation of the mother" is la Malinche, [Spanish conquistador Hernán] Cortés's interpreter and mistress during the conquest of Mexico. . . . While Spanish accounts refer to her as "Doña Marina" or "Marina," indigenous Mexicans refer to her as "la Malinche," a name that implies the mythical persona as much as the historical woman. In "Marina/Malinche: Masks and Shadows," Rachel Phillips tries to deflate this myth as much as possible by using the small amount of historical documentation available to reconstruct a more factual account of Marina's life. To begin with, while historians and contemporaries idealize Marina, identifying her as an "Indian Princess," Phillips shows that although she was from an indigenous Mexican tribe, she was far from royalty. Born in Painala, she grew up speaking Nahuatl and was either sold or given away as a child; therefore, she was enslaved by another tribe and moved to Tabasco, where she learned to speak Mayan.

As a young woman, she was given to Cortés, along with nineteen other Indian slave women, as gifts from local Indian leaders. When [the Aztec emperor] Monteczuma's envoys came to Tabasco to find out information about Cortés, they spoke only Nahuatl while Cortés's Spanish translator spoke only Mayan. Marina was used to provide the missing link by translating the Nahuatl into Mayan. Marina soon learned Spanish and became Cortés's primary translator. Contemporary paintings and accounts show that Marina was near Cortés at all times and that her skill as a translator helped him defeat Monteczuma, furthering the cause of the Spanish conquest in Mexico. In addition to her role as translator, historical writings confirm that Cortés and Marina had a sexual relationship; she gave birth to his son, Martin. The last bit of information available about Marina is that some time after this birth, on an expedition to Honduras, Cortés gave her to one of his captains, Juan Jaramillo, to marry. . . .

. . . Malinche embodies both the passivity and violation associated with the fallen woman while simultaneously representing the powerful act of treason as one who [in the words of Luis Leal] "betrays the homeland by aiding the enemy." Both Malinche's betrayal and her violation threaten the Mexican concept of the Male; she either openly challenges his authority or is not saved by his protection. This dual threat makes her the symbol of the female sexuality that is both denigrated and controlled in Mexican society.

The work of a Chicana writer is threatened in a different way by the la Malinche archetype, a way that makes the role model of la Virgen de Guadalupe just as dangerous. For Cisneros, the dilemma is creating a role model for herself and other Chicanas that is neither limited by this good/bad duality ingrained in Mexican culture, nor too "Anglicized" to adequately represent their experience. When interviewing Cisneros, Pilar E. Rodriguez-Aranda observes, "the in-between is not ours. . . . So if you want to get out of these two roles, you feel you're betraying your people." In response to this dilemma, Cisneros claims that she and other Chicana women must learn the art of "revising" themselves by learning to "accept [their] culture, but not without adapting [themselves] as women."

The House on Mango Street is just such an adaptation. The author "revises" the significance of the Chicana archetypes of la Malinche and la Virgen de Guadalupe through her characterization of females in the book. By recasting these mythical stories from the female perspective, Cisneros shows how artificial and confining these cultural stereotypes are, and through her creation of Esperanza, imagines a protagonist who can embody both the violation associated with la Malinche and the nurturing associated with la Virgen de Guadalupe, all the while rejecting the feminine passivity that is promoted by both role models. Therefore, Esperanza transcends the good/ bad dichotomy associated with these archetypes and becomes a new model for Chicana womanhood: an independent, autonomous artist whose house is of the heart, not of the worshiper, nor of the conqueror.

Maria Elena de Valdes observes that in *The House on Mango Street*, Esperanza is "drawn to the women and girls [in the story] as would-be role models." Not surprisingly, Esperanza does not find many lives that she would like to emulate. Her rejection of these role models stems from each character's close alliance with one of the two Mexican archetypes. Cisneros shows how being culturally defined by either of these two roles makes for an incomplete, frustrated life. While the Virgin Mother is a venerated role model, Cisneros complicates this veneration through her characterization of other maternal figures, most notably, Esperanza's mother and her aunt, Lupe.

In "Hairs," Cisneros paints an intimate picture of Esperanza's relationship with her mother, whose hair holds "the smell when she makes room for you on her side of the bed still warm with her skin, and you sleep near her." Like the Virgin, Esperanza's mother is a protector, a haven for her daughter during the rain. This idealized memory is marred somewhat in "A Smart Cookie," in which it is clear that Esperanza's mother is very talented, that she can "speak two languages," and "can sing an opera," but that she is not contented with her life. Mother says, "I could've been somebody, you know?" Apparently, being the nurturing, self-sacrificing mother whose hair "smells like bread" is not sufficient to make Esperanza's mother's life complete. Instead of being a dependent female, Esperanza's mother tells her daughter that she has "[g]ot to take care all your own," alluding to a culture that desires virgin-like women, but which does not reward the desired passivity with the care and adoration also reserved for the Virgin; instead, Mother mentions several friends who have fulfilled their roles as mothers but have consequently been left alone. Mother encourages her daughter to reject this self-sacrificing path that Mexican culture sees as noble, like the Virgin, and to choose instead to "study hard" in school in order to prepare herself for independence.

A more forceful rejection of the Virgin archetype is evident in the characterization of Esperanza's aunt, Guadalupe. Like the mythic character for whom she is named, Aunt Lupe is a passive woman in a shrine, but in "Born Bad," this connection is corrupted with images of sickness, stagnation, and helplessness. Unlike Paz's assertion that "through suffering, our women become like our men: invulnerable, impassive and stoic," there is nothing idyllic or positive about Cisneros's portrayal of a suffering woman. Instead of living in a resplendent holy place, Cisneros's Guadalupe lives in a cramped, filthy room with "dirty dishes in the sink" and "ceilings dusty with flies." The passivity of Lupe is the result of a debilitating illness that has caused her bones to go "limp as worms." Guadalupe is chaste like the Virgin, but her lack of sexual activity is

The author suggests that Cisneros shows that the traditional female role models of la Virgen de Guadalupe and la Malinche produce lives of hardship and imprisonment of various kinds. Copyright © Glowimages RM/Alamy.

not a sign of her moral superiority; it is again caused by her illness and associated with the frustration and longing of "the husband who wanted a wife again." . . .

While the primary female characters associated with the Virgin in *The House on Mango Street* are adult figures, and therefore distant and revered, the females aligned with la Malinche are adolescents, making them more accessible to Esperanza in her search for role models. The images of la Malinche are more widespread in Cisneros's book than those of the Virgin; in fact, images of the violated, abandoned, or enslaved woman are scattered from beginning to end, indicating that the unfortunate reality of Malinche/Marina's life is a more likely scenario for women in the barrio than that of being worshipped as the ideal mother. Rosa Vargas, a woman with unruly children, "cries every day for the man who left without even leaving a dollar"; the abandonment seems to be the reason she is such a distracted, ineffective mother. The husband of another character, Rafaela, locks her "indoors because [he] is afraid [she] will run away since she is too beautiful to look at." In this story, Rafaela, like Malinche, is enslaved because she and her sexuality are viewed as threats that must be contained. . . .

While all of these women represent aspects of the Malinche archetype, perhaps the most sustained exploration of that archetype in *The House on Mango Street* can be found in the character of Marin, who, like Aunt Lupe, shares the name of the mythical figure she represents. By reading Marin's story through the lens of the la Malinche archetype, one gains insight into the pitfalls of this culturally proscribed role. In "Louie, His Cousin & His Other Cousin," the description of Marin immediately aligns her with the darker, more sexual side of Chicana femininity; she wears "dark nylons all the time and lots of makeup" and is more worldly than Esperanza and the other girls. Like Malinche, Marin is living with people who are not her family, and in a sense, she is enslaved; she "can't come out—gotta baby-sit with Louie's sisters."

It is Marin's aspirations, however, that most closely align her with Malinche. Marin says that,

> she's going to get a real job downtown, because that's where the best jobs are, since you always get to look beautiful and get to wear nice clothes and can meet someone in the subway who might marry you and take you to live in a big house far away.

Like Malinche, Marin could be perceived as betraying her family and culture. By "getting a job downtown," she is leaving her neighborhood and her duty as babysitter to go where the "better jobs" are, in the more Anglo-oriented downtown area. However, Marin does not see her actions as an act of betrayal; she is hoping for self-improvement. Just as Malinche's position as translator for the powerful Cortés seems logically preferable to being a slave who "kneads bread" for those in her own country, Marin's desire to escape her circumstances are justifiable. But, for Marin, and Malinche, this escape is inextricably tied to dependence on a man. The dream of marriage and a "big house far away" are Marin's sustaining thoughts, but the reality of her focus on sexuality leads to a denigration much like that of Malinche. While Marin believes that "what matters . . . is for the boys to see us and for us to see them," this contact only provides a space for lewd sexual invitations from young men, who "say stupid things like I am in love with those two green apples you call eyes, give them to me why don't you." Finally, Marin, like Malinche, is sent away because "she's too much trouble."

Through these connections, Cisneros's text appropriates the Malinche myth, showing that this type of dependence on men for one's importance and security is what leads to violation and abandonment. The danger of Marin's "waiting for . . . someone to change her life" lies in the possible result of this passivity. Paz comments on this potential for downfall: "This passivity, open to the outside world, causes her to lose her identity: she is the Chingada. She loses her name; she is no one; she disappears into nothingness; she is Nothingness. And yet she is the cruel incarnation of the feminine condition." Cisneros seems to suggest that this "nothingness" is almost inevitable for women in the barrio.

Perhaps no one in *The House on Mango Street* more fully embodies the "cruel incarnation of the feminine condition" than Esperanza's friend, Sally. At different times in the book, Sally can be aligned with both la Malinche and la Virgen de Guadalupe, and her story reveals both the objectification and confinement associated with each archetype. In "Sally," her description, like Marin's, suggests a link with physical sexuality and desirability. She has "eyes like Egypt and nylons the color of smoke," and her hair is "shiny black like raven feathers." Unfortunately, Sally's attractiveness is the source of much unhappiness. Because her looks are perceived as a sign of promiscuity, she is stigmatized in her school; the boys tell stories about her in the coatroom, and she has very few female friends. More damaging, though, is the reaction of her father, who "says to be this beautiful is trouble," and confines Sally to her room. Like la Malinche, Sally's sexuality is doubly threatening to her father's masculinity. Not only could she betray him by being promiscuous, but her beauty might also entice a man to violate her, which would threaten the father's role as protector. This perceived threat causes her father to erupt in horrific displays of violence, hitting his daughter until her "pretty face [is] beaten and black" because "[h]e thinks [she's] going to run away like his sisters who made the family ashamed." Sally's father uses force to deform her and to contain her threatening sexuality.

To get away from her father's abuse, Sally marries a marshmallow salesman, "young and not ready but married just the same." Sally "says she's in love, but . . . she did it to escape." Sally perceives marriage as the path for leaving behind the "bad girl" image that links her to la Malinche as well as the violence she associates with this connection. As a wife she gains respectability and a propriety of which her culture approves; her sexuality has been contained within the proper confines of marriage, and now she has the potential to recreate the Virgin's role as nurturer and worshipped love.

In "Linoleum Roses," Cisneros again juxtaposes the reality of the female situation with its mythic counterpart. Significantly, the image of the "linoleum roses on the floor" echoes the story of Juan Diego's flowers that heralded the need for a house of worship for the Virgin. Similarly, Sally's roses are proof of her status as a "good" female. Like the Virgin, Sally gets the home that she wants, but again the house functions more like a prison than a shrine. As Julian Olivares argues, the linoleum roses are a "trope for household confinement and drudgery, and an ironic treatment of the garden motif, which is associated with freedom and the outdoors." Sally "sits at home because she is afraid to go outside without [her husband's] permission," Her only consolation is looking at the roses and the other "things they own." Sally has not gained much from her crossing from one extreme to the other of the good/bad dichotomy that classifies Chicana women. The house of her husband is just as limiting as the house of her father. . . .

The most obvious connection made between Esperanza and either of these archetypes is the protagonist's desire for a house, which resonates with la Virgen de Guadalupe's charge to Juan Diego that "they build my temple for me here." In "Bums in the Attic," Esperanza, like the Virgin, wants "a house on a hill like the ones with the gardens." Esperanza's hill is connected to the hill of Tepeyac, the location of la Virgen de Guadalupe's shrine, and the reference to the garden is easily associated with the flowers on the hill that the Virgin made grow as a sign of her divinity. Perhaps a more significant connection between the Virgin and Esperanza is Esperanza's plan for her house:

> One day I'll own my own house, but I won't forget who I am or where I came from. Passing bums will ask, Can I come in? I'll offer them the attic, ask them to stay, because I know how it is to be without a house.

Esperanza's promise to take care of the bums is important for two reasons. First, it echoes the Virgin's promises to give "aid and . . . protection" to her followers, and to "hear their weeping . . . and heal all . . . their sufferings, and their sorrows." Furthermore, Esperanza promises not to forget "where [she] came from," establishing a connection with her society that is reminiscent of the Virgin's position as the "truly Mexican" symbol. While some critics mistakenly interpret Esperanza's desire for a house as a betrayal of her heritage that is more in line with the negative aspects of the la Malinche myth, her attitude toward the "bums" shows that she is not blind to the needs of those in her community, nor will she neglect her responsibility to that community. Although Esperanza's desire for a house is prompted by her desire for security and autonomy, it also encompasses a degree of compassion and nurturing that represents the noblest qualities of the Virgin archetype. . . .

It is Esperanza's dream for a house, a dream inextricably linked with her poetry, that keeps her from succumbing to her culture's demand that she be identified with one of these archetypes. Olivares interprets Esperanza's house as a "metaphor for the house of storytelling." In such a metaphorical space, Esperanza can create for herself an identity that reconciles the violation and pain that she associates with Mango Street as well as the responsibility she feels to nurture and aid her community, the place in which she "belong[s] but do[es] not belong to." Esperanza imagines:

> One day I will pack my bags of books and paper. One day I will say goodbye to Mango. I am too strong for her to keep me here forever. One day I will go away. Friends and neighbors will say, What happened to that Esperanza? Where did she go with all those books and papers? Why did she march so far away? They will not know I have gone away to come back. For the ones I left behind. For the ones who cannot out.

Elements of la Malinche and the Virgin are fused in Esperanza's plan. Like Malinche, Esperanza goes off into the world of the "conqueror," the more affluent, anglicized society outside the barrio, and also like Malinche, her motivations will be questioned. However, like the Virgin, Esperanza will return to support, protect, and aid those that need her within the barrio. Esperanza imagines herself as a bridge between these two worlds, and her writing is the tool that helps her create this connection: "I make a story for my life." According to Wendy Kolmar, the "vision at the end of *The House on Mango Street* can only be achieved by the narrative's resistance of boundaries, separations, and dualisms," and the most significant dualism that Esperanza rejects is the division of "good" versus "bad" females in her culture. Esperanza is neither "good" nor "bad"; she encompasses traits of both the Virgin and la Malinche, but she refuses passively to accept the label of either one. Instead, she sees her life, like her dream house, as a space "clean as paper before the poem," with potential for creativity, autonomy, and most importantly, self-definition. . . .

Childish Play Inspires Esperanza's Creative Responsibility

Stella Bolaki

Stella Bolaki is a postdoctoral research fellow in the Institute for Advanced Studies in the Humanities at the University of Edinburgh in Scotland, where she researches poetics and narratives of illness and disability.

In the following selection, Bolaki explores the contradictions in the works of ethnic women. On the one hand is community responsibility; on the other is the need to break free. Bolaki focuses on the link between the young narrator's childish play in the House on Mango Street *stories and the joy she takes in her creativity as an adult writer. Bolaki dismisses the argument that Cisneros's playful approach to literature renders the work politically insignificant or irresponsible. Cisneros, herself, counters that charge by claiming that she is being realistic about women in the barrio. In Esperanza's playfulness and games, Bolaki asserts, she casts off the typical role assigned to girls by men. Furthermore, Bolaki argues that Esperanza's transition into adulthood is less about leaving behind her childhood and more about claiming her creative and political responsibilities.*

Esperanza negotiates a balance between the demands of her community and her need for a space of creativity and pleasure not only through writing, . . . but also through playing. The notion of "play" that I advance here is situated between the literal, in other words the actual games of Esperanza and her friends, and the metaphorical, that is, the ways in which play is understood as an artistic practice. . . .

Stella Bolaki, "More Room to Play in Sandra Cisneros's *The House on Mango Street*," *Journal of American Studies of Turkey*, vol. 23, 2006, pp. 65–74. Reproduced by permission.

The Vision of a Child

In many ways, an artist shares "the child's instinct for fantasy; the free play between its imaginings and the world of fact.... Whether it becomes associated with children or with artists, however, play is often seen in opposition to reality or to serious work. Children are not expected to contribute to society.... Despite the nostalgia with which adults view childhood, there is, nevertheless, the expectation that children will grow up and take a socially responsible position in the adults' world. Similarly, an artist's only possible work is art, but when reduced to free play and formal experimentation it risks being dismissed for promoting an aestheticism that has no practical value. Thus, artists, especially minority ones, are also expected to grow up by making their art more mature....

As I want to show, playing has a ... function in *The House on Mango Street*. Like writing, playing is "stubborn" not only because the text is interspersed with games, but also because games continue for Esperanza longer than is necessary. Although games in *The House on Mango Street* become an occasion to interact with other people and thus are not as private as Esperanza's practice of self-talk, they, too, refer to a potentially "heretical" space of enjoyment, which allows one to maintain distance from the properly social.... In "The Monkey Garden" Esperanza describes such a space of freedom and autonomy. As she explains, the children "took over the garden" when the monkey that used to live there moved, and from then on used to go to the garden because it was "far away from where our mothers could find us." The garden presents an alternative to some of the stifling domestic settings in *The House on Mango Street*. With its "dizzy bees", "the sleepy smell of rotting wood", "weeds like so many squinty-eyed stars", and with "flowers that stopped obeying the little bricks that kept them from growing beyond their paths," it is presented as a locus of enjoyment.... Esperanza likes this place because "[t]hings had a way of disappearing in the garden, as if the garden itself ate them". On one occasion a child fell asleep under a tree while playing a game and disappeared "until somebody remembered he was in the game and went back to look for him". As Esperanza notes, "This is where I wanted to die."

Esperanza Resists Adulthood

Does this precocious fascination with death demonstrate a stubborn determination not to grow up, a fantasy of never leaving childhood? The garden, after all, with its "big green apples" and which gives the impression that it has "been there before anything," gathers echoes of the Garden of Eden and brings in mind the myth of Childhood as Paradise Lost. At first glance, Esperanza seems to want to prolong this dimension of her life, to retain the child in her. To the suggestion for instance that she is too old to play games, she responds, "Who was it that said I was getting too old to play the games? Who wasn't it I didn't listen to?" . . .

Esperanza's friend Sally also seems to be prone to acts of *Extravagance* which could be dismissed as frivolous. Esperanza describes Sally as a woman who is in pursuit of her own enjoyment, too: "Sally is the girl with eyes like Egypt and nylons the color of smoke . . . her hair is shiny black like raven feathers and when she laughs, she flicks her hair back like a satin shawl". The language of this passage with its descriptive extravagance heightens such an effect. . . . Esperanza asks Sally to join her: "I said, Sally, come on, but she wouldn't. She stayed by the curb talking to Tito and his friends. Play with the kids if you want, she said, I'm staying here". Sally's comment not only signals a division between the world of adults and that of children but also differentiates between the kinds of games that are appropriate for boys as opposed to those that are prescribed for girls. Sally stays by the curb, immobile, while Esperanza wants "to run up and down and through the monkey garden, fast as the boys, not like Sally who screamed if she got her stocking muddy".

Esperanza prefers to continue playing "with the kids" rather than participating in Sally's game. . . .

On the contrary, Esperanza's games open different paths and thus allow her to maintain distance from limiting scripts of femininity. This is not to say, however, that Esperanza does not try out more traditionally "feminine" games. . . .

Playing and Writing

Many *vignettes* align the children's games with linguistic games. Games provide for Esperanza a kind of laboratory to conduct her experiments with language, a space which complements the private space of creativity that she longs for, that is, the house. In a *vignette* entitled "Hips", Esperanza's formation as a writer is anticipated through an immediate connection of language and play. Drawing on their thoughts about a physical change in their bodies, Esperanza and her friends participate in a creative exercise; while they dance or jump the rope, each one improvises a little poem about the meaning of hips:

Some are skinny like chicken lips.

Some are baggy like soggy band-aids

After you get out of the bathtub.

I don't care what kind I get.

Just as long as I get hips.

The scene could be dismissed as trivial or as an example of the reason why female culture, a culture of "children-women", is susceptible to charges of worthlessness. . . . However; the pleasure derived from the game is not a pure waste of energy. The game depends on the contribution of each player and promotes collaboration. The outcome of the song the girls create, unlike the same song that Marin sings in order to attract the boys, a private pleasure absorbed by patriarchy, is "not totally assimilable to the model of normative het-

erosexuality" [according to literary critic Geoffrey Sanborn].
Its product is of a different kind; work and play seem to coexist in this game, which, to recall us of Sanborn's phrase . . .
can be seen as "recreational, in the strong *re-creational* sense
of the word" (my emphasis). The distinction between this
type of creative Work and "real" work becomes evident
through the sharp contrast between this *vignette* and the one
that directly follows, entitled "The First Job". This *vignette*
starts with a sense of guilt on the part of Esperanza—"It
wasn't as if I didn't want to work"—and ends with an account
of sexual abuse in the workplace. Unlike the game described
in the previous *vignette*, work in "The First Job" takes the
form of a series of uncreative and repetitive duties, which allow no room for personal feeling.

The game in "Hips" is not, nevertheless, totally free in the
sense of undisciplined; it has its own rules, but these are voluntarily adopted. Only Nenny, Esperanza's younger sister, cannot follow them. She does not seem to be able to move away
from the kids' usual rhymes while, as Esperanza explains, the
purpose of the game is to invent something new:

> Not that old song, I say. You gotta use your own song. Make
> it up, you know? But she doesn't get it or won't . . . Nenny, I
> say, but she doesn't hear me. She is too many light years
> away. She is in a world we don't belong to anymore. Nenny.
> Going. Going. . . .

In *The House on Mango Street* in particular, as I hope to
have shown, Esperanza glimpses in the childhood experience
of playing, which becomes transmuted into playful writing,
the possibility of a creative *and* politically responsible adjustment to the complex world she inhabits.

Esperanza Develops in Spite of Two Oppressive Cultures

Gale Joyce Bellas

Gale Joyce Bellas, a teacher at Fairfield University in Connecticut, is best known for her book A Dialogic Approach to Reading and Teaching Ethnic American Texts, *in which she discusses works by Simon Ortiz, Sherman Alexie, and Toni Morrison, among others.*

Bellas's view in the following excerpt is that Esperanza is a part of two cultures: the Chicano culture of her family and neighbors as well as the dominant white culture. Bellas asserts that Esperanza's narrative is an attempt to create her own identity by blending elements of both cultures. But Esperanza refuses to romanticize her own childhood and ends up rejecting the male-dominated world that surrounds her. Although she meets with prejudice and stereotypes from the dominant culture because of her economic status and ethnicity, she comes to realize that gender inequality and the repression of women operate more brutally in her own Chicano culture than in the mainstream. This is particularly true in the case of the motherless Alicia who, although she goes to university, is completely under the control of and terrorized by her father. Outside of her neighborhood, Esperanza finds less sexism and the opportunity for a woman to be free and fulfilled. Bellas observes that when Esperanza confronts the two cultures' prejudices and balances her existence within them, she has created a brand new path for Chicana women.

Gale Joyce Bellas, "Homes of the Heart," in *A Dialogic Approach to Reading and Teaching Ethnic American Texts*, Lewiston, NY: The Edwin Mellen Press, 2006, pp. 45–54. Copyright © 2006 Gale Joyce Bellas. All rights reserved. Reproduced by permission.

In *The House on Mango Street*, Cisneros uses storytelling as a vehicle for Esperanza's voice. Her stories serve several major purposes. First, they define and shape boundaries between her individual self and the Chicano and dominant white cultures. Readers can hear how Esperanza, a schoolgirl whose family resides in the Latino section of Chicago, defines and shapes boundaries by the way she reacts to beliefs within these cultures. Second, her stories attempt to connect these various voices and pieces to form a sense of unity within Esperanza so that she can make sense of certain experiences or situations. Her stories help her to resist a disenfranchised and splintered self that may result from belonging to both cultures but not entirely to one or the other. Esperanza attempts to connect to her environment(s) from which she feels disconnected. Ironically, the more stories she tells, the more she begins to enter a new place that is rooted within herself, rather than in an external environment. By the end of her narrative, Esperanza defines the house that she wants to own one day as "a house of the heart." . . . Esperanza represents the power of choice, or at least the power of envisioning choice by subscribing to certain values from both cultures. . . .

Negotiating Two Cultures

Both narrative and self are shaped in relation to the voices within her Chicano culture and the dominant culture.

Esperanza literally shapes a unique self through an active dialogue with multiple voices as she negotiates and creates her own polyphonic space among them. In *Masterpieces of Latino Literature*, [critic] Frank Magill contends that "Esperanza wants to re-create herself from scratch and create the house, too, that will reflect and define her." In her dialogue, one can hear those voices she either rejects or collaborates with while she filters them through her own unique imagination. One of the first voices the reader hears belongs to a nun who teaches at the Catholic school Esperanza attends. In the first chapter of her narrative, she reacts to a conversation she has with the nun from school when she lived on Loomis Street prior to her family moving to Mango Street. The nun gets lost in Esperanza's neighborhood and bumps into Esperanza on the street. When Esperanza points to her house, the nun replies, "You live there?" . . .

The nun's words signal a prevalent bias within the dominant culture that judges people by their economic status. Esperanza is, of course, embarrassed by the nun's harsh words and does not know how to react since she has not yet developed a discourse of her own to counteract the nun's. All Esperanza knows is that it makes her "feel like nothing." From the nun's comments, the reader gets an indication early on of the nature of the conflict and hardship Esperanza will attempt to overcome.

Although the image of her ideal house changes as her narrative progresses, the very first image the reader gets of what kind of house Esperanza wants is revealed in the following passage:

> And our house would have running water and pipes that worked. And inside it would have real stairs, not hallway stairs, but stairs inside like the houses on T.V. And we'd have a basement and at least three washrooms so when we took a bath we wouldn't have to tell everybody. Our house would be white with trees around it, a great big yard and grass growing without a fence. This was the house Papa talked about when he held a lottery ticket and this was the house Mama dreamed up in the stories she told us before we went to bed.

Here we have an example of how Esperanza negotiates the diverse voices from her own and the dominant culture in an attempt to create her own discourse. Esperanza creates the image of her ideal house in response to several factors. First, her image is partially constructed in reaction to the inequity within the dominant culture, which defines individuals by where they live. She reacts to the nun's assessment of her living situation—"You live there?"—and is made to feel embarrassed by where she lives. Secondly, her image is a product of the types of houses she sees on television: white houses with big yards that exist in suburban America. Thirdly, her image is derived from her desire to live comfortably. She wants a house with pipes that work and three bathrooms so she does not have to share a bathroom with her entire family. And finally, Esperanza is reacting to her and her parents' hope to acquire a piece of the American Dream and how her faith in this dream is lessened by the fact that her family did not win the lottery and, therefore, ended up buying a house on Mango Street. . . .

Inequality in Her Own Culture

Esperanza's narrative "proclaims its difference" not only in the way she reacts to certain voices within the dominant culture, but also in the way she reacts to certain voices within her own culture. In her discussion in "Boys and Girls," she says,

> The boys and the girls live in separate worlds. The boys in their universe and we in ours. My brothers for example. They've got plenty to say to me and Nenny inside the house. But outside they can't be seen talking to girls.

Early on in her narrative, Esperanza establishes the inequity between boys and girls in her neighborhood. Even though she does not have a name for this inequity, she realizes that it exists.

Throughout her narrative, Esperanza maintains her commentary about the rigidly defined gender roles that exist within her community and the inequities these roles bring about. In "Alicia Who Sees Mice," there is another reference to the inequality of fixed gender roles in the Chicano culture that assign women to the position of men's caretakers:

> Alicia, whose mama died, is sorry there is no one older to rise and make the lunch box tortillas. Alicia, who inherited

81

> her mama's rolling pin and sleepiness, is young and smart
> and studies for the first time at the university. Two trains
> and a bus because she doesn't want to spend her whole life
> in a factory or behind a rolling pin. Is a good girl, my friend,
> studies all night and sees the mice, the ones her father says
> do not exist. Is afraid of nothing except four-legged fur. And
> fathers.

The status of women in her culture is clearly defined in this passage. Men inherit money or houses, and land, while women inherit "rolling pins" and "sleepiness." The use of voice found in this passage is almost a reversal of the use of voice found in Esperanza's recreation of her encounter with the nun from her school. Here, Esperanza rejects a prominent aspect of her own culture and collaborates with an aspect of the dominant culture. The aspect of the Chicano culture she rejects is the expectation that a woman's role is to serve her man. The aspect of the dominant culture she collaborates with is the acceptance of a woman receiving an education, and thus, being able to choose her role in life. Esperanza shows a growing concern for women in her community who have decided that their fate has already been sealed and give up on possible alternatives. Moreover, her narrative is concerned with the opportunities that education could provide for Chicano women. Since economic freedom is necessary for control over one's life, Esperanza sees education as an opportunity for Chicano women to gain their independence.

Inequality Within the Larger, White Culture

A theme that also reoccurs throughout her narrative, is the racial prejudice displayed by the white culture towards the Hispanic culture. In "Those Who Don't," Esperanza addresses this prejudice by explaining what happens when people of different economic classes leave their own neighborhoods:

> Those who don't know any better come into our neighborhood scared. They think we're dangerous. . . . They are stupid people who are lost and got here by mistake.

In The House on Mango Street, *Esperanza records her impressions of life in her barrio, and we see it through her eyes.* Copyright © Ken Weingart/Alamy.

But we aren't afraid. . . .

> All brown all around, we are safe. But watch us drive into a
> neighborhood of another color and our knees go shakity-
> shake and our car windows get rolled up tight and our eyes
> look straight. Yeah. That is how it goes and goes.

Perhaps Esperanza sees the dominant culture as an opportunity for certain economic and social benefits that she feels are
not offered within her own culture. Yet, at the same time, Esperanza realizes the racial and class boundaries that exist
within American society.

Although Esperanza wishes to escape the confines placed
upon her by her Chicano community, she wishes to remain
connected to certain aspects of this community when she
leaves. In "Bums in the Attic," Esperanza explains that when
she moves away from her neighborhood, she will take in bums
from the street and let them live in her attic. The bums will
serve as a reminder of where she has come from. In the final
chapter, she also states that when she leaves, "They will not
know I have gone away to come back. For the ones I left behind. For the ones who cannot out." This passage reflects the
hardships she is faced with as a modern Chicana: she does not
wish to participate in the racial or class discrimination prevalent in the dominant culture, nor does she wish to be a victim
of the gender discrimination and lack of economic opportunity within her own culture. Yet, at the same time, she wishes
to maintain a degree of her Chicananess.

In the penultimate chapter, "A House of My Own," Esperanza finds her own space, so to speak, by rejecting particular
voices from both the dominant culture and her own culture
that attempt to objectify her.

Resistance and Alienation

It is Esperanza's resistance to certain values from both the
dominant and Chicano cultures that empowers Esperanza as

her narrative takes shape. Her choosing between both cultures, however, also results in feelings of alienation. . . .

Esperanza feels the difficulties of belonging to two worlds, which she does not wholly feel a part. Throughout her narrative, she shares this sentiment of not belonging with others in her neighborhood who she clearly sees do not belong either. In the chapter "No Speak English," Esperanza describes a woman, Mamacita, who recently moved to the United States. She cannot speak English and is made fun of by her husband and the children in the neighborhood. . . .

Esperanza's compassion for Mamacita suggests that Esperanza also feels like Mamacita: a foreigner in her own neighborhood. In "Four Skinny Trees," Esperanza even compares herself to trees in the neighborhood that look out of place.

> They are the only ones who understand me. I am the only one who understands them. Four skinny trees with skinny necks and pointy elbows like mine. Four who do not belong here but are here.

The process of identification with trees rather than people shows Esperanza's isolation and her desire to leave the reality that exists around her. She goes on to say,

> Their strength is their secret. They send ferocious roots beneath the ground. They grow up and they grow down and grab the earth between their hairy toes and bite the sky with violent teeth and never quit their anger. This is how they keep . . . Four who grew despite concrete. Four who reach and do not forget to reach.

This discussion of the four trees is really a discussion of how Esperanza views herself in relation to her environment(s). She feels out of place, like the trees, yet she realizes that strength is the secret to their survival in a place where they do not belong. . . .

Her voice resists the objectification of women and the economic poverty she finds within her own neighborhood and the prejudice and stereotypes imposed upon her by the dominant culture. Esperanza suffers a feeling of alienation from her own culture and the consequences of replanting herself as a new entity. She is blazing a trail for a new Chicano woman as she attempts to overcome the sexism, diminishing opportunities and value on education within her own community, and the racism present in the dominant American culture.

Esperanza Claims Her Identity Through Education and Writing

Julián Olivares

Julián Olivares, a professor of modern and classical languages at the University of Houston, is the author and editor of numerous journals and books, including Women's Lyric Poetry of the Golden Age.

Olivares asserts in the following selection that Esperanza's poverty and ethnicity place her outside the mainstream white society in her adolescent years, and her gender places her outside the power structure within her own culture. But her aunt advises her that she will be liberated from the gender barrier by her writing. Unlike most other girls she knows, Esperanza determines to escape the patriarchy of her culture. In Olivares's view, the five major topics treated in The House on Mango Street *are all related to gender roles or the lives of girls and women in the barrio: stories about family, usually focused on women and girls; stories of sexual awareness; stories of gender subjugation, abuse, and abandonment; stories of identity; and stories about writing, which will liberate Esperanza from the barrio's patriarchy.*

Sandra Cisneros's *The House on Mango Street* is a book about Esperanza Cordero, a Chicana girl who lives in the barrio, or ghetto, of a large city. Through forty-four brief lyrical narratives, or vignettes, as Cisneros has called them . . . , ranging from one-half to three pages, the girl recounts her growth from puberty to adolescence within the sociopolitical frame of poverty, racial discrimination, and gender subjuga-

Julián Olivares, "Entering *The House on Mango Street*," in *Teaching American Ethnic Literatures: Nineteen Essays*, edited by John R. Maitino and David R. Peck, Albuquerque, NM: University of New Mexico Press, 1996, pp. 209–27. Copyright © 1996 by the University of New Mexico Press. All rights reserved. Reproduced by permission.

tion. The book's action is propelled by three major themes: the girl's desire to find a suitable house (essentially a move away from the barrio), to find her identity, and to become a writer. Identity is crucial, for it not only means coming to terms with her Latino ethnicity, but also arriving at a gender consciousness not circumscribed by the gender determinants of her culture. Consequently, the narrator is "twice a minority"; she is doubly marginated because of her ethnicity and her patriarchal society. As we will ascertain, the themes are inextricably interrelated; the resolution of the themes of house and identity is to be achieved by her role as writer.

The House on Mango Street is a book about growing up, what critics call a bildungsroman. This genre is cultivated commonly in the United States by emerging writers, often first- or second-generation immigrants, and especially within literatures emerging around the periphery of a dominant society. It offers the advantage of a first-person narration that becomes the basis for the expression of subjectivity; the protagonist relates his or her experiences in the growth from childhood to maturity, the latter determined by the dialectic with culture and society. . . .

Liberations Through Writing

The house on Mango Street is an extension of Esperanza Cordero's identity. While not as dilapidated as her previous house on Loomis Street, for her, its poor state is a sign of her poverty and shame. As her character develops in the work and she becomes more aware of her gender constraints, the wish for a pretty house becomes a desire for unfettered female space. At the conclusion, the house becomes a metaphor for the space of writing.

Esperanza Cordero is clearly conscious of self-exploration through writing. In the first half of the book, the reader has the impression of overhearing the protagonist "tell" stories. As the stories proceed, her growth and character development are signaled by her language development and her heightened poetic imagery. In the dialogue Esperanza relates with her aunt in "Bad Girl," the twenty-third piece, the protagonist reveals that she writes poetry, and with the subsequent stories it becomes clear that these are the memoirs she has written of her first year's experience of living in the barrio, in the little red house on Mango Street: "You live right here, 4006 Mango, Alicia says and points to the house I am ashamed of. No, this isn't my house I say and shake my head as if shaking could undo the year I've lived here." It is through writing, as her aunt tells her, that Esperanza will achieve her social and gender liberation. . . .

The initial piece is representative of *Mango Street*'s form, voice, and style. The form is a prose poem; the narrating presence is a composite of a poetic enunciating voice and a narrative voice. The style is consistent with that of a young girl speaking idiomatic English, with colloquialisms and a few Spanish expressions—a deceptively simple but richly imagistic language. The personification of the house is typical of a child's way of seeing and inventing the world, but it also points to the influence of story books and initiates a series of allusions to fairy tales that will appear throughout the book. However, these tales will be subverted. In this case, the rural red house is moved to a large city ghetto; and it is red (only in children's stories are houses red) because it is made of red bricks, but these bricks are crumbling. The personification creating this defamiliarized fairy-book atmosphere functions, in turn, to underscore the shared identity of dilapidated house and dejected inhabitant.

The second piece, "Hairs," briefly describes the family and reveals that although externally the house is a picture of poverty, inside there is warmth and communion. "Boys and Girls," the third narrative, posits the theme of gender difference, the need to find a girlfriend to overcome her loneliness—"Until then I am a red balloon, a balloon tied to an anchor"—and begins the exposition of the narrator's world.

The desire to live in a beautiful house is concomitant to finding another identity. But the identity she seeks must be freed from the gender oppression of her culture. In "My Name," the fourth piece, Esperanza says: "In English my name means hope. In Spanish it means too many letters. It means sadness, it means waiting. . . . It is the Mexican records my father plays on Sunday mornings when he is shaving, songs like sobbing." In this lyrical sketch, Esperanza traces the reason for the discomfiture with her name to cultural hegemony, the Mexican males' suppression of their women. . . .

Five Categories About Gender

The stories Esperanza relates fall into five categories, many of which are interrelated:

1. The family, children, and the barrio: "Hairs," "Our Good Day," "Laughter," "Gil's Furniture Bought & Sold," "Meme Ortiz," "Louie, His Cousin & His Other Cousin," "Those Who Don't," "Darius and the Clouds," "And Some More," "A Rice Sandwich," "Chanclas," "Papa Who Wakes Up Tired in the Dark," "Geraldo No Last Name," "The Earl of Tennessee," "A Smart Cookie."

2. Sexual awareness: "The Family of Little Feet" "Hips," "The First Job," "Sire," "Minerva Writes Poems," "The Monkey Garden," "Red Clowns."

3. Child and gender oppression, abuse, and abandonment: "Cathy, Queen of Cats," "Marin," "There Was an Old Woman She Had So Many Children She Didn't Know What to Do," "Alicia Who Sees Mice," "The First Job," "Born Bad," "No Speak English," "Rafaela Who Drinks Coconut & Papaya Juice on Tuesdays," "Sally," "Minerva Writes Poems," "A Smart Cookie," "What Sally Said," "The Monkey Garden," "Linoleum Roses," "Red Clowns."

4. Identity: "The House on Mango Street," "My Name," "Elenita, Cards, Palm, Water," "Four Skinny Trees," "Bums in the Attic," "Beautiful and Cruel," "The Monkey

Garden," "The Three Sisters," "A House of My Own,"
"Mango Says Goodbye Sometimes."

5. Writing—pieces intrinsically related to the discovery of
identity: "Born Bad," "Edna's Ruthie," "Minerva Writes
Poems," "The Three Sisters," "A House of My Own,"
"Mango Says Goodbye Sometimes." . . .

The Girls' Sexual Awareness

The physical changes that mark the transition from puberty
to adolescence are signs confirming female identity, bringing
with it an awareness of sexuality. However, Esperanza's exhila-
ration in arriving at this stage of physical development is
offset not only by her encounters with the dangers that sexuality provokes, but also with her awareness of the gender proscription that is set in place once sexuality becomes manifest.
Esperanza's first encounter with sexual danger is the conse-
quence of a typical and innocent game played by young girls.
In "The Family of Little Feet," Esperanza and her friends
put on cast-off high heels and take delight in pretending to be
adult women. The corner grocer perceives the sexual danger
that the high heels signal and tells the girls to take them off:
"Them are dangerous, he says. You girls too young to be wearing shoes like that." As they flee from the grocer, his admon-
ishment is realized when, first, a boy, in typical male sexual
banter, calls out to them, "Ladies, lead me to heaven"; and,
second, in their encounter with male sexual aggression when
a drunk asks one of the girls to come closer—"Your little
lemon shoes are so beautiful. But come closer. I can't see very
well"—and tells her he'll give her a dollar for a kiss. The girls
run away in their high heels and take them off because they
"are tired of being beautiful." In this episode with allusions
to "Little Red Riding Hood," Cisneros, as she does with
fairy tales, deflates a light-hearted reading of a typical child's
dressing-up episode in order to focus on the girls' introduction to a sexual power structure that they only dimly perceive. . . .

In adolescence, Esperanza is attracted by what she perceives to be the romantic and liberating aspects of her sexuality, only to learn that it exposes her to peril and male domination. In "Sire," she relates her burgeoning sexuality, her attraction to boys, and her desire to escape from a child's confinement and to sit outside at night like a "bad girl": "Everything is holding its breath inside me. Everything is waiting to explode like Christmas. I want to be all new and shiny. I want to sit out bad at night, a boy around my neck and the wind under my skirt. Not this way, every evening talking to the trees, leaning out the window, imagining what I can't see." "Red Clowns," however, brutally undermines her romantic notions of love and sex. Her physical coming-of-age is tragically confirmed by physical violation. . . .

Gender Roles Are Deromanticized

In "Alicia Who Sees Mice," Venus—and the implication of sex and marriage as escape—is deromanticized, is eclipsed by a cultural reality that points to the drudgery of gender confinement. Alicia "is young and smart and studies for the first time at the university. Two trains and a bus, because she doesn't want to spend her whole life in a factory or behind a rolling pin. . . . Is afraid of nothing except four-legged fur. And fathers."

Most of the girls and young women in *Mango Street*, however, cannot aspire to an education; rather, they want to grow up fast and get married. But these, like Minerva, usually have to get married, and they leave a father for a domineering husband. Such is the fate of Sally in "Linoleum Roses." . . .

In "The Three Sisters," three old Women appear at the *velorio* (wake) of a neighbor's baby. To Esperanza, their presence is a mysterious one: "They came with the wind that blows in August, thin as a spider web and barely noticed. Three who did not seem to be related to anything but the moon." Like the *curandera* ["witch woman" and healer] and the aunt, these women appear at critical junctures to advance the narrative and to assist the heroine in her quest. Unlike the two previous stories, however, the sisters' intervention is related in the combination of the characteristic prose-poem form with an extended dialogue sequence. On the level of the plot, the elderly sisters, who appear like fairy godmothers, bring revelation and the gift of self to Esperanza.

Writing and Gender

The three sisters . . . appear on the symbolic level as the Three Fates who determine the heroine's destiny and leave her with the prophecy of self-knowledge. Esperanza has received her wish, but does not understand it. How can she leave and still be Mango Street? How can she come back for the others? What is the meaning of the circle? Esperanza thought that by leaving Mango Street and living in another house, one that she could point to with pride, she would leave behind forever an environment she believed to be only temporary. Three mysterious women embed in Esperanza's psyche a cultural and political determination that will find expression in her vocation as a writer. Esperanza eventually will move away from the confining space of house and barrio, but paradoxically, within them she has encountered the liberating space of writing.

Through her creativity, Esperanza comes to inhabit the house of storytelling. The material house of her own—"Not a flat. Not an apartment in back. Not a man's house. Not a daddy's. A house all my own. With my porch and my pillow, my pretty purple petunias. My books and my stories. My two shoes waiting beside the bed. Nobody to shake a stick at. Nobody's garbage to pick up after"—lies in the future. What Esperanza can have now, however, is a magical house entered through the door of her creative imagination. . . .

Cisneros's *The House on Mango Street*, like . . . other works by Chicano authors pronounces the counterdiscourse of a minority people; yet, at the same time, it responds to these works' cultural ideology of Hispanic male supremacy. As [critic] Yvonne Yarbro-Bejarano lucidly points out: "Esperanza is painfully aware of the racial and economic oppression her community suffers, but it is the fate of the women in her barrio that has the most profound impact on her, especially as she begins to develop sexually and learns that the same fate might be hers. Esperanza gathers strength from the experience of these women to reject the imposition of rigid gender roles predetermined by her culture." As we have noted, Esperanza's escape from her physical and cultural confinement is achieved through education and writing. Determined not to wind up like the victimized women of her barrio, she does encounter a few positive role models who encourage her education and writing.

The rejection of her culture's gender proscription, achieved through writing, also entails moving away from the barrio to her own female space, a move that could be incorrectly perceived by some as a rejection of her class; but Esperanza concludes her text with the promise to return: "They will not know I have gone away to come back. For the ones I left behind. For the ones who cannot out."

Cisneros's slender but powerful fiction departs from the paradigm of the traditional female bildungsroman, which submits to the literary and ideological hegemony of masculine discourse. In her coming-of-age literary testimony, Esperanza refuses to accept her expected position in society. This determination is not only manifested by her actions—"I have begun my own quiet war. Simple. Sure. I am one who leaves the table like a man, without putting back the chair or picking up the plate"—but by the empowering act of writing. [As Yarbro-Bejarano puts it,] "She seeks self-empowerment through writing, while recognizing her commitment to a community of Chicanas. Writing has been essential in connecting her with the power of women and her promise to pass down that power to other women is fulfilled by the writing and publication of the text itself". . . .

The House Represents Women's Limitations and Liberation

Alvina E. Quintana

Alvina E. Quintana, professor of English and women's studies at the University of Delaware, is the author of Reading United States Latina Writers *and* Home Girls.

In the following excerpt, Quintana reads The House on Mango Street *as a radically new feminist text within Chicano literature in which Sandra Cisneros undermines the male-centered patriarchy so ingrained in Chicano life. Cisneros, through her young narrator, examines the reality of her community—a community that has "inherited" social injustices, Quintana argues. Through her narrative, Cisneros shows that she is interested in not just Esperanza's challenge of and escape from the patriarchy, but also the plight of all women in the barrio. The houses on Mango Street, including Esperanza's own, represent women's limitations, confinement, and servitude, Quintana notes. But by considering her grandmother in Mexico and the women around her, Esperanza records women's past in a new way, different from the old respectful literature created by males.*

Although the National Association for Chicano Studies had organized annual conventions for eleven years, not until 1984 at the twelfth national conference in Austin, Texas, were scholars sanctioned by the theme of the convention—Voces de la Mujer [Female Voices]—to address issues related to an emergent Chicana feminist movement. . . .

Alvina E. Quintana, *"The House on Mango Street*: An Appropriation of Word, Space and Sign," in *Home Girls: Chicana Literary Voices*, Philadelphia, PA: Temple University Press, 1996, pp. 54–74. Copyright © 1996 by Temple University. All rights reserved. Reproduced by permission.

Not a Traditional Approach

Sandra Cisneros's [*The House on*] *Mango Street* defied the poetic form previously privileged by many Chicana writers. In a text of forty-four poetically charged vignettes centering on women's experiences, Cisneros defined a distinctive Chicana literary space—oh so gently she flung down the gauntlet, challenging, at the least, accepted literary form, gender inequities, and the cultural and economic subordination of minorities. Theoretically speaking, this little text subverts traditional form and content in a way that demonstrates how conventional applications of literary genre and the social construction of gender undermine a "feminist aesthetic." . . .

The House on Mango Street breaks with the traditional bildungsroman [coming-of-age genre] even as it demonstrates how coming-of-age in a patriarchal society shapes a recognition of prescribed gender roles. The freedom and independence associated with male coming-of-age narratives has typically been replaced in the female versions by loss of freedom and acceptance of subordination; the narratives have tended to portray imprisoned, trapped, or isolated women. But *Mango Street's* young heroine escapes isolation and succeeds on "male terms" as she experiences integration and freedom. The book's episodes challenge societal and cultural codes by emphasizing the protagonist's refusal to accept prescribed gender limitations. . . .

Mango Street also subverts conventional literary form, blurring genres and linking poetic vignettes to illustrate the day-to-day experiences and perceptions of Esperanza, an adolescent growing up in a Chicago barrio. Cisneros calls the stories in *Mango Street* "lazy poems," the product of genre fusion. "For me each of the stories could've developed into poems, but they were not poems. They were stories, albeit hovering in that grey area between two genres. My newer work is still exploring this terrain." . . .

Mango's protagonist enables the author to shrewdly introduce a variety of political concerns that confront Chicano/a communities in the United States. Cisneros plays off a tension between the simplicity of the young narrator's point of view and the somber realities she represents, beginning with the title story, which opens the book.

> We didn't always live on Mango Street. Before that we lived on Loomis on the third floor, and before that we lived on Keeler. Before Keeler it was Paulina, and before that I can't remember. But what I remember most is moving a lot.... We had to leave the flat on Loomis quick. The water pipes broke and the landlord wouldn't fix them because the house was too old. We had to leave fast. We were using the washroom next door and carrying water over in empty milk gallons.

Later through Esperanza's reflections, readers become privy to the individual alienation and shame created by her family's plight.

> I want a house on a hill like the ones with the gardens where Papa works. We go on Sundays, Papa's day off. I used to go. I don't anymore. You don't like to go out with us, Papa says. Getting too old? Getting too stuck-up says [her sister] Nenny. I don't tell them I am ashamed—all of us staring out the window like the hungry. I am tired of looking at what we can't have.

Resistance in a Controversial Portrayal

On an ideological level, Esperanza dreams the American dream; on a material level, like all in her community she remains systematically excluded from it.

Even if the views of her protagonist are naive, Cisneros's depiction of Esperanza itself represents a refined challenge to domination. Cisneros's portrayal of the social predicament contributing to her protagonist's confusion is a symbolic act of resistance on the author's part....

The tension becomes more complex when we consider the points of view of author and narrator. The book's tendency to conflate the two perspectives has led some critics to argue that Esperanza's narrative (and, by implication, Cisneros's politics) simply illustrates an individual's desire for a house outside the barrio. This viewpoint fails to regard Cisneros's attempts to distinguish between Mexican cultural tradition and the social injustices Chicano communities have inherited. . . .

As do all rite-of-passage narratives, *Mango Street* represents maturation. Readers witness a subtle shift in the protagonist's understanding as she begins to consider some of the issues contributing to her subordinate cultural position. Yet despite this movement toward self-awareness and sophistication, Esperanza's voice holds echoes of some of her childish, impressionistic perceptions; consequently her visions of success and escape seem limited and naive. In "Geraldo No Last Name," for example, she has difficulty understanding why her friend Marin concerns herself about a hit-and-run victim, a young man she had met at a dance.

> But what difference does it make? He wasn't anything to her. He wasn't her boyfriend or anything like that. Just another *brazer* who didn't speak English. Just another wetback. You know the kind the ones who always look ashamed.

If this is the level of Esperanza's maturation, the extent of her cultural awareness, what are readers to make of the author's point of view? [Critic] Susan Lanser's study of narrative is instructional here; her conceptual model that distinguishes between the point of view of the "real author" and the "narrator" enables us to appreciate Cisneros's narrative quandary. As writer, Cisneros sends a text to her audience. This text combines an authorial voice with a collection of women's voices from the barrio that together create an image for the reader. . . .

Cultural, Social, and Economic Boundaries

Through Esperanza, Cisneros shows readers how class boundaries and ideologies perpetuate a world that allows individuals to perform their social roles without considering the real conditions of their existence. Like other female members of poor ethnic communities, Esperanza suffers the inevitable consequences of race, class, and gender oppression. In her, the representative of a class of marginalized and subsequently alienated individuals, Cisneros shows "real" readers the limitations of an ideology that simply envisions liberation in individualistic terms. She advances her social critique by exposing a variety of barrio experiences.

In the fourth story, "My Name," it becomes clear that Esperanza wishes to reinvent herself in order to transcend the limitations that result from her ethnic identity. Throughout *Mango Street* she has seemed to feel more embarrassed than angry about her situation; now we hear her innermost thoughts about self-fashioning. . . .

In this story as in other Chicana literature, "grandmother" signifies the symbolic matriarchal handing down of cultural traditions. But Cisneros's Esperanza subverts the usual process, stating, "I have inherited her name, but I don't want to inherit her place by the window." Overturning the customary nostalgic sentiment that associates grandmothers with positive cultural nourishment, Cisneros's great-grandmother represents "traditional, cultural values" as confining and debilitating. Thus Esperanza wants a culturally uncoded new name—Zeze the X.

By providing a critique of the "traditional" Mexican female experience, Cisneros's stories serve as an ethnographic allegory of female humanity, for they "simultaneously describe real cultural events and make additional moral, ideological, and even cosmological statements." Through the words of her young protagonist, Cisneros has made a precarious start on a project of cultural critique. [Poet] Adrienne Rich calls this kind of writing "Revision—the act of looking back, of seeing with fresh eyes, of entering an old text from a new critical direction." It is, Rich says, "for women more than a chapter in cultural history: it is an act of survival. Until we understand the assumptions in which we are drenched we cannot know ourselves." Rich argues that women cannot reenvision themselves without first having a clear understanding of the past; and they must know it differently than they have ever known it, in order not to pass on a tradition but to break its hold over them. "Thus, a feminist rewriting of literature would begin first by examining how women have been living, how they have been led to imagine themselves, how the very act of naming has been till now a male prerogative."

Since Esperanza's reflections in "My Name" begin by considering the cultural implications of naming itself, what seems to reflect an internally oppressive state . . . can, if we are influenced by Rich's thinking, instead be viewed as a healthy step toward self-actualization. Cisneros illustrates how Esperanza's name, which in "English . . . means hope," is quickly distorted to mean a "sadness and waiting," a dramatic shift in meaning predicated on gender, culture, and class oppression. Readers here witness an ideological shift that transforms the noun *esperanza* (hope) into the verb *esperar* (to wait), we see that Esperanza's most personal experiences are determined by outside forces. Esperanza does not control her own destiny; she is a passive agent acted upon by a system beyond her control. . . .

Mango Street depicts Esperanza's internalized oppression, a state of mind prompted by her belief in the American dream and her desire for the escape that assimilation offers. In "Alicia and I Talking on Edna's Steps," Alicia, recognizing Esperanza's self-contempt, counsels her to remember who she is and where she came from. . . .

Esperanza, frustrated because her desires and her material reality seem inconsistent, reconciles her feelings by expressing shame and discontent. . . .

The House as Women's Limitations

Through Esperanza's characterization, Cisneros depicts some of the inner conflicts that develop as marginalized individuals attempt to resolve the apparent disjunction between their desires for cultural integrity and for individual liberation.

The symbol Cisneros chooses to represent the ideological, cultural, and economic limits imposed on the marginalized woman's space is the house. For Esperanza, life becomes a struggle to secure individual success and, her ultimate aspiration, a house of her own, a home unlike her family's, which is "small and red with tight little steps in front and windows so small you'd think they were holding their breath. Bricks are crumbling in places, and the front door is so swollen you have to push hard to get in." Esperanza longs for a house like the one in her mother's bedtime stories, "white with trees around it, a great big yard and grass growing without a fence." . . .

On a material level one's house symbolically reflects one's success and achievement to the outside world. Yet in more figurative terms, the word denotes the domestic sphere, a metonomy [symbol] for women's space. To the private/public dialectic Cisneros adds yet another opposition: insider/outsider cultural values, the political implications of the dominant cultural system of the United States as well as the internal convictions emphasized by Mexican culture. House becomes the metaphor for success and escape from the limitations imposed on Chicanas by cultural traditions, as well as for the boundaries and limitations of poverty. . . .

Cisneros defies tradition by writing about censored topics and in the process demonstrates Adrienne Rich's point about women's writing. Cisneros revises history by honestly confronting her past. She has embraced an assertive role, sculpting cultural impressions that have helped refine Chicana feminist aesthetics. Many of her vignettes dwell on the mundane and unromantic activities of women. "There Was an Old

Woman She Had So Many Children She Didn't Know What to Do" inscribes the simple life of a single mother. . . .

Bringing Women to the Center

Cisneros's sophisticated critique of patriarchal control employs the simple language of an adolescent coming to terms with female dailiness in her community and constructs the foundation for a counterdiscourse. Her literary project is similar to historian Bettina Aptheker's. Confronting the absence of women in traditional historical accounts, Aptheker sets out to develop alternative approaches to conventional historiography, among them an examination of women's everyday experiences.

> By the dailiness of women's lives I mean the patterns women create and the meanings women invent each day and over time as a result of their labors, and in the context of their subordinated status to men. . . . The point is to suggest a way of knowing from the meanings women give to their labors.

Both Aptheker and Cisneros are engaged in discursive projects that bring women from the margins to the center, recognizing them as active participants in history rather than pawns struggling for self-expression and escape.

Cisneros portrays the options available to women by presenting both positive and negative female role models and constructs a mosaic of common problems to convey not only women's struggles but also their tactics for conflict resolution. Mexican cultural practices maintain a system that classifies women according to their marital status; one is viewed either as a *señorita* (virgin) or as a *señora* (sexually active wife), a polarity that constantly forces women to define themselves as accessories to men. A woman who steps outside these acceptable roles finds herself classified according to a masculine interpretation of history, she is viewed as a *puta*, that is as a harlot or sexual deviant. . . .

Trapped in a Space of Male Dominance

The media's representational practices seduce women into thinking that their very existence depends on how successfully they prepare themselves for the male gaze. Sally's dilemma is that what enhances her attractiveness to "the boys" arouses her father's disapproval and concern; her placement between her father's expectations and the boys' desire renders her powerless. Women are caught in the double bind created by masculine anticipation and experience; recognizing their confinement in this gender-determined space, they develop the desire for freedom and self-control.

In the title character in "Marin," Esperanza's Puerto Rican friend, Cisneros depicts a conventional female strategy based solidly in a dominant (male) ideology. Accepting her inferior and powerless position as a woman in a man's world, Marin dreams of escaping from poverty. . . .

Because Marin is both a native of Puerto Rico and a woman, her tactics for advancement combine the influences of both identities. Cisneros's portrayal of her suggests a parallel between the aspirations of a woman who has accepted a subordinate position based on gender inequality and those of a colonized subject. Even as a U.S. colony, Puerto Rico continues to use Spanish as its official language. . . .

In one short passage in the next story, "Alicia Who Sees Mice," Cisneros does not merely describe the limitations of patriarchal systems but writes about the tension between the past and the future, posing a solution that could enable women to transcend a cultural legacy of "lunchbox tortillas" and "a woman's place." . . .

Because *Mango Street* can be read from a variety of non-threatening positions, it has been used in many universities as a primer for raising consciousness about gender oppression; it seems to challenge patriarchal institutions and cultures gently, from an apparently middle-class, mainstream perspective. Closer reading, however, reveals the voice of innocence and naiveté as a narrative strategy that allows the author to construct a safe space from which, paradoxically, she can expose the existential estrangement that derives from cultural and economic subordination. The narrative thus functions as the ultimate strategy for escape from confining traditions. Cisneros enables her readers to look critically at the assumptions that engulf them.

Cisneros Builds on Symbols of Other Female Writers

Jacqueline Doyle

Jacqueline Doyle, professor of English at California State University–East Bay, has written on Sandra Cisneros and Puerto Rican author Judith Ortiz Cofer.

In the following selection, Doyle explores the similarities and differences between Cisneros's view of a woman's space in The House on Mango Street *with the view of early twentieth-century English novelist Virginia Woolf, who wrote of a woman's space in her essay* A Room of One's Own, *published in 1929. Woolf's "room" is equivalent to Cisneros's "house of her own," Doyle asserts. While Woolf writes from the perspective of a wealthy, upper-class white woman, Cisneros writes from the perspective of a poor, ethnic-minority woman. Ironically, Doyle writes, for most of the women in Cisneros's work, houses are prisons. Women are closely confined in these structures, which belong to and are run for and by men. Doyle observes that the dangers girls and women face come from within their own neighborhoods and houses. The house Esperanza will build from her heart will be her own, not her father's.*

Cisneros's *The House on Mango Street*, dedicated in two languages "A las Mujeres/To the Women," both continues [Virginia] Woolf's meditations and alters the legacy of *A Room of One's Own* in important ways. Her series of vignettes is about the maturing of a young Chicana and the development of a writer; it is about the women she grows up with; it is also about a sense of community, culture, and place. Esperanza, the young protagonist, yearns for "a space for myself to go, clean as paper before the poem," and for a house of her own:

Jacqueline Doyle, "More Room of Her Own: Sandra Cisneros's *The House on Mango Street*," *MELUS*, vol. 19, no. 4, Winter 1994, pp. 2–15. Copyright © MELUS: The Society for the Study of Multi-Ethnic Literature of the United States, 1994. Reproduced by permission.

Not a flat. Not an apartment in back. Not a man's house.
Not a daddy's. A house all my own. With my porch and my
pillow, my pretty purple petunias. My books and my stories.
My two shoes waiting beside the bed. Nobody to shake a
stick at. Nobody's garbage to pick up after. . . .

The Difference Poverty Makes

The dilapidated series of apartments and houses Esperanza inhabits with her mother, father, sister, and two brothers—
particularly their dwelling on Mango Street—represents her
poverty, but also the richness of her subject matter. "Like it or
not you are Mango Street," her friend Alicia tells her, "and one
day you'll come back too." "You must remember to come
back," the three aged sisters tell her, "for the ones who cannot
leave as easily as you." *A Room of One's Own* would seem to
allow Esperanza this subject, even to encourage it. "All these
infinitely obscure lives remain to be recorded," as Woolf told
her young female audience. Pondering the shopgirl behind the
counter, she commented, "I would as soon have her true history as the hundred and fiftieth life of Napoleon." But Woolf's
class and ethnic biases might also deter Esperanza from achiev-
ing her own literary voice.

Cisneros's *The House on Mango Street* covertly transforms
the terms of Woolf's vision, making room in the female literary tradition for a young working-class Chicana who "like[s]
to tell stories": "I make a story for my life," Esperanza tells us,
"for each step my brown shoe takes. I say, 'And so she trudged
up the wooden stairs, her sad brown shoes taking her to the
house she never liked.'" If Esperanza's name means "too many
letters," means "sadness" in the life she knows in Spanish, it
translates as "hope" in English. Thinking back through her
mothers and their comadres and across through her sisters,
she builds her house from the unfulfilled hopes and dreams
around her. "I could've been somebody, you know?" sighs her
mother. Edna's Ruthie next door "could have been [many
things] if she wanted to," muses Esperanza, but instead she got

married to a husband nobody ever sees. Esperanza inherited her name from her great-grandmother, a "wild horse of a [young] woman" who, tamed by marriage, spent her days confined in her husband's house. "She looked out the window all her life," says Esperanza: "I wonder if she made the best with what she got or was she sorry because she couldn't be all the things she wanted to be. Esperanza. I have inherited her name, but I don't want to inherit her place by the window." As Esperanza revises and lays claim to her matrilineal inheritance, so Cisneros in *Mango Street* offers a rich reconsideration of the contemporary feminist inheritance as well. . . .

Dickinson and Cisneros

In a tribute to the "essential angel" of her own childhood, Cisneros has acknowledged the importance of Woolf's belief that a room of one's own is a necessary precondition for writing. Allowing her room of her own, Cisneros's mother enabled her daughter to create: "I'm here," Cisneros explained to an audience of young writers, "because my mother let me stay in my room reading and studying, perhaps because she didn't want me to inherit her sadness and her rolling pin." In "Living as a Writer," Cisneros again stresses that she has "always had a room of [her] own": "As Virginia Woolf has said, a woman writer needs money, leisure, and a room of her own." Elsewhere Cisneros indirectly questions the class bias of Woolf's perspective, however, when she discusses her early "dream of becoming a writer" and the inspiration of Emily Dickinson as a female literary precedent for her poetry. "What I didn't realize about Emily Dickinson," Cisneros told a junior high audience, "was that she had a few essentials going for her":

> 1) an education, 2) a room of her own in a house of her own that she shared with her sister Lavinia, and 3) money inherited along with the house after her father died. She even had a maid, an Irish housekeeper who did, I suspect, most of the household chores. . . . I wonder if Emily

Dickinson's Irish housekeeper wrote poetry or if she ever had the secret desire to study and be anything besides a housekeeper.

Tribute to a Range of Women

As Woolf speculated on Shakespeare's hypothetical, silenced sister, Cisneros speculates on Dickinson's housekeeper, comparing her to her own mother, "who could sing a Puccini opera, cook a dinner for nine with only five dollars, who could draw and tell stories and who probably would've enjoyed a college education" if she could have managed one. In *The House on Mango Street*, Esperanza's mother tells her that she herself should never have quit school. "Study hard," she tells her daughter, stirring the oatmeal, "Look at my comadres. She means Izaura whose husband left and Yolanda whose husband is dead. Got to take care all your own, she says shaking her head."

Woolf stressed the importance of a female tradition for the woman writer: "we think back through our mothers if we are women." For both Alice Walker and Sandra Cisneros, these mothers include women outside the "tradition" as it is conventionally understood, women who, perhaps anonymously, "handed on the creative spark, the seed of the flower they themselves never hoped to see; or . . . a sealed letter they could not plainly read." Esperanza's mother—her encouragement, but also what she has not written, not expressed—is central to the community of female relationships informing her daughter's development as an artist. Esperanza's tribute to her mother, "A Smart Cookie," opens: "I could've been somebody, you know? my mother says and sighs." Her list of talents—"She can speak two languages. She can sing an opera. She knows how to fix a T.V."—is framed by her confinement in a city whose subway system she has never mastered, and extended in a list of unfulfilled desires. . . . Esperanza's mother points to the girl's godmothers (her own comadres, or, literally translated, "comothers," powerful family figures in Chicano culture) as examples of the necessity "to take care all your own." In the extended filiations of her ethnic community Esperanza finds a network of maternal figures. She writes to celebrate all of their unfulfilled talents and dreams and to compensate for their losses.

Cisneros loosely structures her series of prose pieces as a Kunstlerroman [a story of the coming of age of an artist], whereby the final piece circles back to the opening. Esperanza's closing statement, "I like to tell stories. I am going to tell you a story about a girl who didn't want to belong," is followed by a repetition of the opening lines of the book that she is now able to write. The paired sections opening and closing the book strongly evoke Esperanza's maternal muse. While the opening chapter describes their ramshackle series of third-floor flats and the unsatisfactory house on Mango Street where Esperanza has no room of her own, her mother's body in the second chapter provides all of the security and warmth and "room" that the small girl desires. . . .

A House of One's Own

The two closing sketches, "A House of My Own" and "Mango Says Goodbye Sometimes," describe the grown Esperanza's ideal house of her own where she can create, "a space for my-self to go, clean as paper before the poem," and also her new relation to Mango Street and her origins. The house on Mango Street becomes an overtly maternal figure who collaborates in her freedom and creativity: "I write it down and Mango says goodbye sometimes. She does not hold me with both arms. She sets me free." . . .

A Room Can Be a Prison

In story after story of the women in her community, Esper-anza recognizes that a room—if not of one's own—can be sti-fling.

Her own grandmother, unhappily married, "looked out the window all her life, the way so many women sit their sad-

English writer Virginia Woolf. The author asserts that Cisneros continues Woolf's reflections from A Room of One's Own *and changes the view of rooms to suit Esperanza's Latina experience.* AP Images.

ness on an elbow." Because Rafaela is beautiful, her husband locks her indoors on Tuesday nights while he plays dominoes; Rafaela is "still young," Esperanza explains, "but getting old from leaning out the window so much." Louie's cousin Marin "can't come out—gotta baby-sit with Louie's sisters—but she stands in the doorway a lot." "We never see Marin until her aunt comes home from work," Esperanza tells us, "and even then she can only stay out front." Across the street on the third floor, Mamacita, who speaks no English, "sits all day by the window and plays the Spanish radio shows and sings all the homesick songs about her country." Sally's father keeps her inside and beats her when he thinks of his sisters who ran away. Later Sally's husband won't let her talk on the phone or even look out the window:

> She sits at home because she is afraid to go outside without his permission. She looks at all the things they own: the towels and the toaster, the alarm clock and the drapes. She likes looking at the walls, at how neatly their corners meet, the linoleum roses on the floor, the ceiling smooth as wedding cake.

Dangers from Within and Without

As Rachel, Lucy, Esperanza, and Nenny grow, this sense of community shifts. The dangers that threaten them come from without but also within their own neighborhood, even within their own households. Men's names appear far less frequently in the latter part of Esperanza's narrative, where women's names and the bonds between women predominate. Alicia is "young and smart and studies for the first time at the university," but her father defines her reality and her "place" when he insists that she is "just imagining" the mice in the kitchen and that "anyway, a woman's place is sleeping so she can wake up early with the tortilla star." Rafaela's husband locks her in. Sally becomes a "different Sally" when she hurries "straight home after school," where her father beats her "just because [she's] a daughter." Minerva's husband leaves her "black and blue," and though she "cries" and "prays" and "writes poems on little pieces of paper" she remains trapped in the "same story," the same cycle of violence. Esperanza and her girl-friends successfully flee the bum who wants to kiss them, but already Rachel, "young and dizzy," is tempted by the "sweet things" he says and the dollar in his pocket, and "who can blame her." Later Esperanza endures the unwanted kiss of the "older Oriental man" at her first job, and the brutal sexual assault at the fair where she waits in vain by the grotesque red clowns for Sally. "Why did you leave me all alone?" Sally's escape from the violence of her father's household leads to a new form of confinement and a husband who sometimes "gets angry and once he broke the door where his foot went through, though most days he is okay." . . .

Esperanza's dream of a house of her own—"Not a man's house. Not a daddy's"—is both solitary and communal, a refuge for herself and for others. . . .

A House Affords Freedom

In Cisneros's reconstruction of Woolf's "room of one's own," Esperanza's "house of my own" simultaneously represents an escape from the barrio, a rejection of the domestic drudgery of "home" ("Nobody's garbage to pick up after"), a solitary space for her creativity, and a communal expression of women's lives. Like her name, her dream of a house is a legacy from her family. "Our house would be white with trees around it," Esperanza explains in the opening chapter, "a great big yard and grass growing without a fence. This was the house Papa talked about when he held a lottery ticket and this was the house Mama dreamed up in the stories she told us before we went to bed." The older Esperanza stops listening to her mother's stories of the house when she begins to develop her own. As she gazes longingly at the houses on the hill, "the ones with the gardens where Papa works," she vows that she'll allow space for bums in the attic when she owns her own house. The house becomes as well an imaginary dwelling—the "home in the heart," "house made of heart" prophesied by the witch woman Elenita—as Esperanza's sympathy for Sally animates her vision of a house "with plenty of blue sky," providing shelter for laughter and imagination: "And you could laugh, Sally. You could go to sleep and wake up and never have to think who likes and doesn't like you. You could close your eyes and you wouldn't have to worry what people said because you never belonged here anyway and nobody could make you sad and nobody would think you're strange because you like to dream and dream." Finally the house for Esperanza becomes a creative refuge, "quiet as snow, a space for myself to go, clean as paper before the poem." Many women in the community help her to arrive there: Edna's Ruthie, who listens when she recites "The Walrus and the Carpenter"; Elenita, who tells her fortune; her Aunt Lupe, who listens to her read library books and her first poems; Minerva, who trades poems with her; the three sisters, who offer her prophecies; and her mother, who encourages her to study. . . .

She will speak for the speechless: for Mamacita, who "doesn't come out because she is afraid to speak English," and whose son grows away from her in America. . . .

She will speak for all the women shut in their rooms: for Rafaela, "who is still young but getting old from leaning out the window so much," for Sally, who "sits at home because she is afraid to go outside without [her husband's] permission," for her great-grandmother Esperanza, who "looked out the window all her life." She will speak for the banished: for Louie's other cousin, who gave all the kids a ride in his yellow Cadillac before the cops took him off in handcuffs, [and] for Marin, whose employers will send her back to Puerto Rico. . . .

She will speak for herself: "I have decided not to grow up tame like the others who lay their necks on the threshold waiting for the ball and chain." Instead, like the four trees "who grew despite concrete," "four who reach and do not forget to reach, Esperanza survives to reach for her own freedom and to release the stories of those around her.

The House on Mango Street Is Marginalized Within the Literary Community

Ellen McCracken

Ellen McCracken, a professor in the Department of Spanish and Portuguese at the University of California–Santa Barbara, is the author of numerous books on Latin American culture and literature.

In the following selection, McCracken examines why the literary establishment has been reluctant to give serious consideration to The House on Mango Street, *despite its popularity in schools. The book, she asserts, is marginalized by its ideology, its language, its writer's and protagonist's ethnicity, and their gender. Furthermore, the work refuses to romanticize the lives of Chicana women who are virtually imprisoned in their houses in the traditional male-dominated Latino society, writes McCracken. Cisneros presents starkly realistic views of girls and women subject to the dominating, even violent, patriarchy in the barrio that will never regard them as independent adults and will never stop victimizing them, McCracken observes. Women are purely sexual objects and chattel, doing servile labor. McCracken also claims that* The House on Mango Street *fails to be accepted by the literary elite because its focus is on the community, rather than on the individual alone, and because it is written in simple, accessible language.*

Ellen McCracken, "Sandra Cisneros' *The House on Mango Street*: Community-Oriented Introspection and the Demystification of Patriarchal Violence," in *Breaking Boundaries: Latina Writing and Critical Readings*, edited by Asunción Horno-Delgado, Eliana Ortega, Nina M. Scott, and Nancy Saporta Sternbach, Amherst, MA: University of Massachusetts Press, 1989, pp. 62–71. Copyright © 1989 by the University of Massachusetts Press and published by the University of Massachusetts Press. All rights reserved. Reprinted by permission.

How does a book attain the wide exposure that admission to the canon facilitates if it is four times marginalized by its ideology, its language, and its writer's ethnicity and gender? . . .

The specific example to which I refer, Sandra Cisneros' *The House on Mango Street*, was published by a small regional press in 1984 and reprinted in a second edition of 3,000 in 1985. . . .

In bold contrast to the individualistic introspection of many canonical texts, Cisneros writes a modified autobiographical novel, or *Bildungsroman* [coming-of-age genre], that roots the individual self in the broader socio-political reality of the Chicano community. As we will see, the story of individual development is oriented outwardly here, away from the bourgeois individualism of many standard texts. Cisneros' language also contributes to the text's otherness. In opposition to the complex hermetic language of many canonical works, *The House on Mango Street* recuperates the simplicity of children's speech, paralleling the autobiographical protagonist's chronological age in the book. Although making the text accessible to people with a wider range of reading abilities, such simple and well-crafted prose is not currently in canonical vogue.

The House and the Migrant

On the surface the compelling desire for a house of one's own appears individualistic rather than community oriented, but Cisneros socializes the motif of the house, showing it to be a basic human need left unsatisfied for many of the minority population under capitalism. . . .

For the migrant worker who has moved continuously because of job exigencies and who, like many others in the Chicano community, has been deprived of an adequate place to live because of the inequities of income distribution in U.S. society, the desire for a house is not a sign of individualistic acquisitiveness but rather represents the satisfaction of a basic human need. Cisneros begins her narrative with a description of the housing conditions the protagonist's family has experienced. . . .

Cisneros has socialized the motif of a house of one's own by showing its motivating roots to be the inadequate housing conditions in which she and others in her community lived. We learn that Esperanza, the protagonist Cisneros creates, was subjected to humiliation by her teachers because of her family's living conditions. "You live *there?*" a nun from her school had remarked when seeing Esperanza playing in front of the flat on Loomis [Street in Chicago]. "*There.* I had to look where she pointed—the third floor, the paint peeling, wooden bars Papa had nailed on the windows so we wouldn't fall out. You live *there?* The way she said it made me feel like nothing . . ." Later, after the move to the house on Mango Street that is better but still unsatisfactory, the Sister Superior at her school responds to Esperanza's request to eat lunch in the cafeteria rather than returning home by apparently humiliating the child deliberately: "You don't live far, she says . . . I bet I can see your house from my window. Which one? . . . That one? she said pointing to a row of ugly 3-flats, the ones even the raggedy men are ashamed to go into. Yes, I nodded even though I knew that wasn't my house and started to cry . . ." The Sister Superior is revealing her own prejudices; in effect, she is telling the child, "All you Mexicans must live in such buildings." It is in response to humiliations such as these that the autobiographical protagonist expresses her need for a house of her own. Rather than the mere desire to possess private property, Esperanza's wish for a house represents a positive objectification of the self, the chance to redress humiliation and establish a dignified sense of her own personhood. . . .

Cisneros Does Not Romanticize

[One] important reason why Cisneros's text has not been accepted as part of the dominant canonical discourse is its demystificatory presentation of women's issues, especially the problems low-income Chicana women face. Dedicated "A las Mujeres/To the Women." *The House on Mango Street* presents clusters of women characters through the sometimes naive and sometimes wise vision of the adolescent protagonist. There are positive and negative female role models and, in addition, several key incidents that focus the reader's attention on the contradictions of patriarchal social organization. Few mainstream critics consider these the vital, universal issues that constitute great art. When representatives of the critical establishment do accord a text such as Cisneros' a reading, it is often performed with disinterest and defense mechanisms well in place.

Neither does *The House on Mango Street* lend itself to an exoticized reading of the life of Chicana women that sometimes enables a text's canonical acceptance. In "The Family of Little Feet," for example, Esperanza and her friends dress up in cast-off high heels they have been given and play at being adult women. At first revelling in the male attention they receive from the strangers who see them, the girls are ultimately disillusioned after a drunken bum attempts to purchase a kiss for a dollar. While capturing the fleeting sense of self-value that the attention of male surveyors affords women, Cisneros also critically portrays here the danger of competitive feelings among women when one girl's cousins pretend not to see Esperanza and her friends as they walk by. Also portrayed is the corner grocer's attempt to control female sexuality by threatening to call the police to stop the girls from wearing the heels. Cisneros proscribes a romantic or exotic reading of the dress-up episode, focusing instead on the girls' discovery of the threatening nature of male sexual power that is frequently disguised as desirable male attention. . . .

Scenes of patriarchal and sexual violence in the collection also prevent a romantic reading of women's issues in this Chicano community. We see a woman whose husband locks her in the house, a daughter brutally beaten by her father, and Esperanza's own sexual initiation through rape. Like the threatening corner grocer in "The Family of Little Feet," the men in these stories control or appropriate female sexuality by adopting one or another form of violence as if it were their innate right. One young woman, Rafaela, "gets locked indoors because her husband is afraid [she] will run away since she is too beautiful to look at." Esperanza and her friends send papaya and coconut juice up to the woman in a paper bag on a clothesline she has lowered; metonymically, [by using objects to represent related but more significant and generalized concepts or phenomena] Cisneros suggests that the sweet drinks represent the island the woman has left [Puerto Rico] and the dance hall down the street as well, where other women are ostensibly more in control of their own sexual expression and are allowed to open their homes with keys. The young yet wise narrator, however, recognizes that "always there is someone offering sweeter drinks, someone promising to keep [women] on a silver string."

The cycle of stories about Esperanza's friend Sally shows this patriarchal violence in its more overt stages. Like Rafaela, the young teenager Sally is frequently forced to stay in the house because "her father says to be this beautiful is trouble." But even worse, we learn later that Sally's father beats her. Appearing at school with bruises and scars, Sally tells Esperanza that her father sometimes hits her with his hands "just like a dog . . . as if I was an animal. He thinks I'm going to run away like his sisters who made the family ashamed. Just because I'm a daughter . . ." In "Linoleum Roses," a later story in the Sally cycle, we learn that she escapes her father's brutality by marrying a marshmallow salesman "in another state where it's legal to get married before eighth grade." In effect, her father's violent attempts to control her sexuality—here a case of child abuse—cause Sally to exchange one repressive patriarchal prison for another. Dependent on her husband for money, she is forbidden to talk on the telephone, look out the window, or have her friends visit. In one of his fits of anger, her husband kicks the door in. Where Rafaela's husband imprisons her with a key, Sally's locks her in with psychological force: "[Sally] sits home because she is afraid to go outside without his permission".

Initiation and Violence

A role model for Esperanza, Sally has symbolized the process of sexual initiation for her younger friend. Two stories in the cycle reveal Esperanza's growing awareness of the link between sex, male power, and violence in patriarchal society. In "The Monkey Garden," Esperanza perceives her friend Sally to be in danger when the older girl agrees to "kiss" a group of boys so that they will return her car keys; ". . . they're making her kiss them," Esperanza reports to the mother of one of the boys. When the mother shows no concern, Esperanza undertakes Sally's defense herself: "Sally needed to be saved. I took three big sticks and a brick and figured this was enough." Sally and the boys tell her to go home and Esperanza feels stupid and ashamed. In . . . anguish, she runs to the other end of the garden and, in what seems to be an especially severe form of self-punishment for this young girl, tries to make herself die by willing her heart to stop beating.

In "Red Clowns," the story that follows, Esperanza's first suspicions of the patriarchy's joining of male power, violence, and sex are confirmed beyond a doubt. She had previously used appellation throughout the first story in the Sally cycle to ask her friend to teach her how to dress and apply makeup. Now the appellation to Sally is one of severe disillusionment after Esperanza has been sexually assaulted in an amusement park while waiting for Sally to return from her own sexual liaison:

Sally, you lied. It wasn't like you said at all . . . Why didn't you hear me when I called? Why didn't you tell them to leave me alone? The one who grabbed me by the arm, he wouldn't let me go. He said I love you, Spanish girl, I love you, and pressed his sour mouth to mine ... I couldn't make them go away. I couldn't do anything but cry ... Please don't make me tell it all.

This scene extends the male violence toward Esperanza, begun on her first day of work, when an apparently nice old man "grabs [her] face with both hands and kisses [her] hard on the mouth and doesn't let go." Together with other instances of male violence in the collection—Rafaela's imprisonment, Sally's beatings, and the details of Minerva's life, another young married woman whose husband beats her and throws a rock through the window—these episodes form a continuum in which sex, patriarchal power, and violence are linked. Earlier, Cisneros had developed this connection in the poem "South Sangamon," in which similar elements of male violence predominate: "he punched her belly," "his drunk cussing," "the whole door shakes/like his big foot meant to break it," and "just then/the big rock comes in." *The House on Mango Street* presents this continuum critically, offering an unromanticized, inside view of Esperanza's violent sexual initiation and its links to the oppression of other women in the Chicano community.

Esperanza Finds Role Models

Cisneros does not merely delineate women's victimization in this collection, however. Several positive female role models help to guide Esperanza's development. Minerva, for example, although a victim of her husband's violence, makes time to write poetry. "But when the kids are asleep after she's fed them their pancake dinner, she writes poems on little pieces of paper that she folds over and over and holds in her hands a long time, little pieces of paper that smell like a dime. She lets me read her poems. I let her read mine".... Minerva succeeds in communicating through her art; exchanging poems with Esperanza, she contributes to the latter's artistic development while at the same time offering a lesson in women's domestic oppression and how to begin transcending it. . . .

Cisneros touches on several other important women's issues in this volume, including media images of ideal female beauty, the reifying stare of male surveyors of women, and sex roles within the family. In an effort to counter the sexual division of labor in the home, for example, Esperanza refuses one instance of women's work: "I have begun my own quiet war. Simple. Sure. I am the one who leaves the table like a man, without pulling back the chair or picking up the plate." Although this gesture calls critical attention to gender inequities in the family, Cisneros avoids the issue of who, in fact, will end up performing the household labor that Esperanza refuses here. This important and symbolic, yet somewhat adolescent gesture merely touches on the surface of the problem and is likely, in fact, to increase the work for another woman in Esperanza's household.

The majority of stories in *The House on Mango Street*, however, face important social issues head-on. The volume's simple, poetic language, with its insistence that the individual develops within a social community rather than in isolation, distances it from many accepted canonical texts. Its deceptively simple, childlike prose and its emphasis on the unromanticized, non-mainstream issues of patriarchal violence and ethnic poverty, however, should serve precisely to accord it canonical status. We must work toward a broader understanding among literary critics of the importance of such issues to art in order to attain a richer, more diverse canon and to avoid the undervaluation and oversight of such valuable texts as *The House on Mango Street*.

Patriarchy in the Contemporary World

A Mexican Mother Is Trapped in an Unfaithful Marriage

Rose Castillo Guilbault

Rose Castillo Guilbault has worked for CBS, NBC, *the* San Francisco Chronicle, *and as a member of the California Community College Board of Governors.*

In the excerpt that follows, Guilbault tells a story from her childhood in Mexico. She explains that in the midst of two unfaithful indiscretions, her father is shameless, unsympathetic to her mother, and threatening to take her daughter for his alone. Meanwhile, her family is unsympathetic toward her wish for a divorce. There seems to be no way out until a distant cousin convinces her to seek a new start in America.

It started with whispers. Then muffled comments behind her back. Eventually the gossip had wound its way through the neighborhood grapevine.

People were talking about my mother and father.

It was my mother's good friend and neighbor María who sat her down.

"There's talk you should know about, María Luisa. It has to do with a woman who also lives in town, not far from here."

My mother paled but sat alert.

The Betrayal Rumor

"People say she's Tito's mistress," María continued. "She has a little boy who could be your daughter's brother. I've seen them with my own eyes."

Rose Castillo Guilbault, "A Door Opens," in *Farmworker's Daughter: Growing Up Mexican in America*, Berkeley, CA: Heyday Books, 2005, pp. 15–20. Copyright © 2005 by Rose Castillo Guilbault. All rights reserved. Reproduced by permission.

My mother did not take María's word even though she was a trusted friend. She searched for a woman with a little boy who looked like me until she saw him with her own eyes.

But that wasn't the cruelest blow. Someone else, somehow, somewhere, had passed on an even more disturbing story. These "friends" pulled my mother aside to inform her "for her own good," of course, that they had heard Tito had been previously married and, even though he was divorced, he maintained close relations with his ex-wife and children. Did she know this?

My mother was stunned. The news of a mistress was certainly unpleasant but this was devastating. Hiding a former marriage and family was a deeply wounding deception. It was like looking into Tito's satchel and finding it empty of the expected curios but overflowing with incriminating letters and films.

What else had he lied about? Had he ever told the truth?

My mother walked around the house like a sleepwalker, glassy-eyed and dazed. I watched with curiosity and concern. Mama was acting differently. But not toward me. Even though she seemed unaware of her surroundings, her light touch and gentle voice reassured me that the cause of her gloom had nothing to do with me.

At night when we'd sit listening to the radio I watched her carefully, her face pale and drawn, staring blankly into space. Her eyes clouded and misted but no tears fell. She looked so sad. If I stayed up as long as possible, I could distract her, make her focus those vacant eyes on me, make her smile. But once I crawled into bed to listen to the radio playing the plaintive music of Agustín Lara or Javier Solís, my body relaxed and, too quickly, I'd fall asleep. On the radio a sweet-voiced singer strummed a guitar, interrupted by the occasional crackle of static. The flickering bare bulb on the shadeless lamp cast an enormous shadow around my mother, surrounding her with a phantom-like glow. Through my drooping lids

I'd see my last image of the night: my mother reaching for the box of cigarettes, lighting the end of one with a long kitchen match. A haze of smoke enveloped her as she crushed one cigarette and lit another. The silence of her chain-smoking was interrupted only by the scratch of match against matchbox.

A Husband's Excuses and Threats

Was I there when he casually walked through the door? I'm certain she told me the story only a couple of times, but it was described with such detail and clarity and still-palpable emotion that I've convinced myself I was an eyewitness.

She had considered all her options and was determined. She was prepared to give him an ultimatum when he walked in.

"You're a stupid woman," was his response. "Why would you want a divorce just for this?"

He hotly denied the mistress and argued he hadn't told her about his marriage and divorce because he knew she would have used it as an excuse to not marry him.

"We waited so long, María Luisa."

"Were you married during all those years we courted?"

He closed his eyes, emitted an exasperated sigh.

"Don't throw away our relationship because of something that has nothing to do with you and me. It was in the past, my past. It doesn't intrude on our lives now."

"You lied to me. How can I possibly ever trust you?"

The fight raged for days. He pleaded, cajoled, reasoned, and finally grew angry and defensive. In a voice as cold and cutting as a machete he said, "All right. You can have your divorce. You're a silly, hysterical woman. I misjudged. I thought you were smart and could be my helpmate and help me succeed in my business. I thought that's what we both wanted. Qué lástima." [What a shame.]

María Luisa simmered furiously but did not respond. Her eyes glowered at this man, her husband, suddenly a stranger. What did she really know about him?

"I'll want to take my daughter." He took careful aim to be certain his weapon made a deep and painful cut into her most vulnerable spot.

"Your daughter? What would you do with her? You can't even stand being around her for very long!"

"It doesn't matter. She belongs to me."

"No! You'll never take her! She's just a little girl; she needs her mother."

"We'll see." Tito turned on his heel and walked out the door.

Divorcées Are No Better than Prostitutes

"You can't be serious, Maria Luisa. There's never been a divorce in our family!" The Corral sisters were horrified.

"Let's be honest: Men play around, but Tito wouldn't leave you." Julia, who had married at seventeen, knew this from personal experience.

"*La gente decente* [decent people] think divorcées are the same as prostitutes," sniffed Teresa, the social climber.

"Our mother will turn over in her grave! She never did like that man you married!" said Hermelinda, the youngest.

"Shut up, all of you! I can't believe you'd rather have me stay in a rotten marriage filled with lies and deception, just so others won't talk? I don't give a damn about *gente chismosa*." [gossiping people]

But she did. She worried that she would be ostracized by the families whose children she wanted me to play with. She worried she'd never be able to remarry. That men would see her as tainted, damaged goods, already used by another. She worried she'd be excommunicated from the church, where divorce was not allowed. Most of all she worried Tito would carry out his threat and take me away from her. She knew that by confronting him about his transgressions she had hurt his ego. She had punished him with the ultimate blow. And now he was like a wounded animal, and he wanted to hurt her.

My generation would create no-fault divorce, but in my mother's time and place a woman was expected to endure whatever her marriage brought. It was considered shocking and unacceptable for a woman to seek a divorce, and what with the church, society, and family stalwartly against it, it took either enormous courage or folly for the woman to follow her moral convictions. These institutions would judge her harshly and always remind her it was she who chose her fall from grace.

A Door Opens to Respect

It was in a muddled state of mind, distracted and upset, that my mother bumped straight into a woman while we were at the marketplace one day. Looking up to apologize, she surprised me by exclaiming, "Rafaela!" The woman turned out to be a distant cousin, one she knew more about from reputation than personal contact. Rafaela was considered a bit of a loose woman in the family. She lived in the United States and traveled back and forth alone. Her own children had grown up and she lived by herself. She was divorced.

My mother hadn't seen Rafaela in years, but soon they were chattering as if it had only been days. My mother invited Rafaela home and, over the course of the evening, poured out her troubles. I noticed it had been a long time since I'd seen my mother so talkative.

"What utter nonsense," Rafaela harrumphed, shaking the henna-colored curls on her head. She wagged a long, lacquered red nail at my mother, saying, "You have every right not to put up with *un hombre sinvergüenza* [a shameless man]. Why the hell should you? Because of your sisters? They're not the ones married to him—and and they're not the ones divorcing him either!"

She groaned impatiently, jumped out of her seat, and strode nervously across the room.

"Now, see? This is exactly what makes me crazy about Mexico. Yes, it's my country; I was born here. But these rules about women are so stupid. That's why I'll never come back."

Rafaela grabbed a cigarette, lit it, and inhaled in one fell swoop. I watched for the smoke to come out, but instead a steam of words shot from her mouth.

"You know I'm divorced. The jerk left me! But in the United States, what do you think?" She stood squarely in front of my mother, hand on one slim hip, eyes dancing with anticipated glee. "*En los Estados Unidos* nobody cares. The son of a bitch—that's English for *hijo de su madre*—is gone. I support myself. I own my house, I own my own business. I'm independent."

Rafaela, who had been thumping her chest with her fingers to make her points, now paused, searching my mother's face for her reaction. My mother seemed transfixed, her mouth slightly agape. I looked from one face to another. I'd never been allowed in such an adult conversation.

"And you know what I get from *los americanos?*" Rafaela stopped dramatically and lowered her voice as she breathed out one word: "Respect."

My mother sat mesmerized, unable to unlock her eyes from Rafaela's confident view of another world.

"María Luisa, you come to California with me. Get out of this cesspool. It'll pull you down and drown you. You're still young. Start a new life in a new country. Both for you, and for your daughter's future."

Rafaela sat down on the coffee table facing my mother and took her hands into her own. My mother bit her lip and tears spilled down her face. Rafaela shook their hands up and down encouragingly. María Luisa responded with a tremulous smile.

Sexual Harassment Is Common in American Society

Lis Wiehl

A New York University law professor, legal analyst, and radio co-host for Fox News, Lis Wiehl is the author of Winning Every Time: How to Use the Skills of a Lawyer in the Trials of Your Life *and* The 51% Minority: How Women Still Are Not Equal and What You Can Do About It.

In the following viewpoint excerpted from the chapter titled "Sexual Harassment" in her book, Wiehl asserts that despite the laws designed to protect them, women are still subject to sexual harassment in a society where the victim is often blamed. Wiehl relates incidents in which she, as a woman lawyer, has been belittled in court by an opposing attorney and, in a social situation, has been physically harassed by a man at a party. The second incident made her feel dirty and guilty, which is a common reaction in such cases. Although legal advancements have been made in the twenty-first century, Wiehl reports that sexual harassment is still rampant. And since the large majority of judges and senior management are men, women are frequently dismissed. For this reason, women rarely take action. Theft and drug possession are stringently punished, yet sexual harassment is given leniency, and whistle blowers are inadequately protected. Wiehl suggests redefining acceptable behaviors in our sexist culture as early as childhood education.

When I was representing the House Democrats during the impeachment of President Clinton, I was the subject of several articles and tabloid TV shows that wanted to know "who the blonde is." The *Washington Post* gave out

Lis Wiehl, "Sexual Harassment," in *The 51% Minority: How Women Still Are Not Equal and What You Can Do About It*, New York, NY: Ballantine Books, 2007, pp. 41–60. Copyright © 2007 by Lis Wiehl. All rights reserved. Reproduced by permission.

"awards" such as "Best Trained Attack Dogs" (to Barney Frank and Bill McCollum), and to me they gave the "Most Want to Be Stranded on a Desert Island With" award. Was I insulted? Not really. Did I feel harassed? No.

But there have been other scenarios where I've felt differently. During my tenure as a federal prosecutor, an opposing lawyer in a criminal case was purposely trying to belittle me by commenting on my appearance and femininity. In that circumstance—trying to put a drug lord in jail—I had no recourse to "come back" at him without demeaning myself in doing so in front of the jury. I had to approach the judge behind the scenes and ask that he put a stop to the defense attorney's belittling comments. In another example, an overtly sexual situation occurred this past summer while on vacation. One night before dinner a male in one of the couples with us sidled up to me at the bar and pressed himself up against me. He was excited to be there, if you know what I mean, and I couldn't get away from him fast enough. I felt dirty, and as though *I* had done something wrong. It wasn't until the next day that I could bring myself to talk about it, and my friends said I should have said something right at that moment and that I was "acting like a typical victim of sexual harassment" by blaming myself and saying I "must have been imagining it." I was shocked at the thought that I was blaming *myself*. Should I have made a scene right then and there and embarrassed him? Can I be sexually harassed when I'm out to dinner with friends? What about street hassling and wolf whistles and ogling? . . .

There's a time and place, and sometimes when it's the wrong time, we might decide it's better to slough it off. Court TV commentator Rikki Klieman recalled, "Once I walked into a courtroom where a judge literally asked me 'to do a pirouette.' Instead of reporting him to some judicial conduct commission, I did the twirl, laughed it off, and then never had anything but good results in front of him for decades. Humor and a smile may have gotten us a long way in the 1970s, but bet your bottom dollar, they still work today."

None of us wants to lose the humor at work or in our lives. We certainly don't want to become a sterile society where we're all walking on eggshells for fear of doing something that can get us sued or thrown in jail. Here, all it takes is a little common sense. . . .

The Rights We Have

Sexual harassment entered the national vocabulary in 1991 when Anita Hill came to Capitol Hill to testify against Clarence Thomas's confirmation for Supreme Court. She alleged that Thomas had made sexual advances to her when she was his assistant, saying things about penises, referring to his sexual prowess, and asking her the bizarre question that was played over and over on the news: "Who has pubic hair on my Coke?"

During her testimony before the all-male congressional committee hearing on October 11, 1991, the Yale-educated lawyer described a hostile work environment while working for Thomas at the Department of Education. An environment in which she, as Thomas's assistant, was allegedly constantly asked out and barraged with sexual talk from her boss. . . .

As we all know, despite Hill's testimony, Clarence Thomas is now one of the nine Supreme Court justices. Whether you believe Hill to be a courageous woman speaking up about a Supreme Court nominee's boorish behavior or, as those who sought to discredit her charged, a vindictive soul seeking fifteen minutes of fame, her congressional testimony opened the way for a national discourse on sexual harassment—and led many companies to establish sensitivity training programs in the hope of eliminating sexual harassment from the workplace.

Two months after Anita Hill testified before the country, U.S. District Court Judge James Rosenbaum made legal history by permitting the case of *Jenson v. Eveleth Mines* to proceed as the first-ever class action suit for sexual harassment. . . .

The story (recently made into the movie *North Country*, starring Charlize Theron) begins in 1975 when Lois Jenson, a single mother on welfare, was hired by Eveleth Mines as part of the company's compliance with affirmative action guidelines. As one of the first four women to enter the man's world of iron mining, she and others were subjected to relentless harassment. They were groped, propositioned, called obscene names, deliberately exposed to hard-core pornography, and physically attacked. Eager to be making a decent wage to support her family, Jenson endured. The four women were barraged by daily torment, including a man repeatedly ejaculating on the clothes stored in one woman's locker, two foremen driving two women into the middle of the woods and ordering them to "service them," and perpetual crotch grabbing. The miners would later call these events "jokes."

In 1984, Lois had had enough; she mailed a complaint to the Minnesota Human Rights department. The following week, her tires were slashed. And the fourteen-year legal fight for justice began. . . .

In early 1992, Lois was diagnosed with post-traumatic stress disorder and stopped working at the mine. In December of that year, the trial began before U.S. district judge Richard Kyle in St. Paul, and five months later he ruled that Eveleth Mines was liable for not preventing sexual harassment and ordered the company to develop programs to educate all employees on sexual harassment. (During trial depositions, the miners had answered such questions as "Is rape sexual harassment?" with "It depends on if she asks for it.") . . .

We now have laws recognizing that every human being is entitled to set boundaries between his or her intimate life and the rest of the world. (I say "his or her" because there have been cases of men being harassed at work by female superiors, but, as with most of the power imbalances discussed in this book, sexual harassment is a problem experienced far more often by women than by men.) Today, of the roughly fifteen thousand sexual harassment complaints investigated each year by the agencies of the Equal Opportunity Employment Commission, 89 percent come from women. . . .

These aren't anomalies limited to law enforcement, sports professions, and the occasional midday stroll past a construction site. There's no such thing as a harassment-free profession. From offices to airlines to politics, the culture of "boys will be boys" permeates every professional environment. Sexual harassment is pervasive in our society, creeping around cubicle corners and jumping across streets every day.

In a survey conducted by the American Association of University Women (AAUW) of 1,632 children between the ages of eight and eleven about their experiences with sexual harassment, 85 percent of girls and 76 percent of boys reported having experienced it, with 31 percent of girls and 18 percent of boys saying that it happened "often." Think puberty is the excuse? The AAUW also found that nearly two-thirds of undergraduate college students say they have encountered some type of sexual harassment while in college and more than one-third of female students say the harassment was physical. More than half of the male students admitted to harassing a female in college, a majority of them saying they did so because they thought it was funny.

The law is about respect. Equal respect. For the benefit of both men and women, the important principle of sexual harassment law in the workplace is simple: *If I'm bothered by your actions, I have the right to tell you so and have you stop. If you continue, I have a right to file a complaint, and if you just don't get it, I have the right to take you to court and make you pay.* But what exactly do the courts consider sexual harassment? According to the EEOC, sexual harassment is defined as follows:

> Unwelcome sexual advances, requests for sexual favors, and other verbal or physical conduct of a sexual nature constitutes sexual harassment when submission to or rejection of this conduct explicitly or implicitly affects an individual's employment, unreasonably interferes with an individual's work performance or creates an intimidating, hostile or offensive work environment.

Such behavior is a violation of Title VII of the Civil Rights Act of 1964. Two distinct types of sexual harassment are recognized by the courts. Quid pro quo sexual harassment takes place when a supervisor or boss makes it known that some type of work benefit—a promotion, a raise, a perk, or simply keeping your job—is dependent on sexual favors or continued tolerance of unwelcome advances, verbal or otherwise. Even a single instance of impropriety can be quid pro quo harassment when the stakes are clear: your job, or some benefit of it, is on the line.

Creation of a hostile environment, the second type, need not involve a supervisor or a boss. Ongoing crudeness, unwanted advances, a steady barrage of dirty jokes, or a workplace decorated in sleazy cartoons and *Hustler* pinups can create a hostile environment. Some courts have upheld a "reasonable woman" standard in determining what makes an environment hostile, recognizing that a woman may feel threatened and upset by things that might not bother a man.

Psychiatrists suggest that some men do this as a way of objectifying women and because they can—or think they can—get away with it. Like rape, sexual harassment is more about power than it is about sex. Victims of severe sexual harassment are said to suffer similar emotional aftereffects as victims of rape, and a climate in which sexual harassment is winked at or tolerated blurs the boundaries and paves the way for actual rape. This was acknowledged by the Department of Defense Task Force on Sexual Harassment and Violence at the Military Service Academies, in a report intended to improve the military's dismal track record of handling these matters. "Harassment is the more prevalent and corrosive problem, creating an environment in which sexual assault is likely to occur," the task force found.

What We Should Demand

Sexual harassment is a nasty thing, which is why our laws are strong and straightforward. Unfortunately, because three out of four federal judges and 95 percent of senior management in this country are men, women are often doubted when they report sexual harassment or, worse, are blackballed or fired. The American Bar Association reports that studies have shown women are often treated differently from men in court proceedings. One such study sponsored by the New York Task Force on Women in the Courts illustrates the recurring theme. The report says, "Cultural stereotypes of women's role in marriage and society daily distort courts' . . . application of substantive law. Women uniquely, disproportionately and with unacceptable frequency must endure a climate of condescension, indifference and hostility." This is particularly vexing, given that less than 1 percent of sexual harassment complaints are false. . . .

Prior to 1991, victims of sexual harassment could claim only back pay and lost wages, and could be reinstated by court order if they had been fired. An amendment to Title VII in that year made it possible for juries to award punitive damages, and to compensate victims for emotional distress, inconvenience, mental anguish, loss of enjoyment of life and the like. That change may explain why, in a 1999 survey conducted by the Society for Human Resource Management, 62 percent of companies offered sexual harassment training to their employees, and fully 97 percent had a written policy.

The EEOC will investigate and initiate legal action on your behalf, though one-third of the cases don't go to trial. Why? There is much pressure to settle, and, as exemplified by the

Inappropriate touching, as portrayed here, is an example of sexual harassment—"behavior that crosses the line of decency and makes someone feel cornered, uncomfortable, or violated." Image copyright © Erwin Wodicka, 2009. Used under license from Shutter stock.com.

Jenson v. Eveleth Mines case, the court system doesn't always treat civil rights plaintiffs with kid gloves. Often, when you've got them dead to rights, EEOC complaints end in negotiation rather than in litigation, resolved by something called a "consent decree." This judicial decree expresses a voluntary agreement between the parties, including an agreement by the defendant to cease activities alleged to be illegal in return for an end to the charges.

Whistle-blowing can be hard and scary—and unfortunately, the Supreme Court recently made it even harder. In *Garcetti v. Ceballos*, the court decided in a 5–4 ruling (with Alito and Roberts in the majority) that the First Amendment does not protect public employees who report misconduct or otherwise try to blow the whistle in the course of doing their official duties. The majority opinion said, however, that public employees would have First Amendment protections if they spoke out as private citizens engaged in what Justice Kennedy called "civic discourse." The upshot is, under this ruling, there could be the strange, if not ridiculous, situation where a whistle-blower would be immune from retaliation if she spoke to a reporter but in jeopardy if she went through official channels. . . .

. . . How do we create a new paradigm in which sexual harassment will someday be unthinkable, something that just isn't done? We have to take a good look at the way we educate our children to perceive themselves and each other and the boundaries that exist between acceptable and unacceptable behavior—and the messages we send them through popular culture.

Unfortunately, too many of today's adults—including teachers and school administrators—grew up in an atmosphere where the victim was blamed, shamed, and silenced. We need to come to a mutual understanding that "no" means no, that "stop" means stop, and that we all have our personal levels of what we're comfortable with. This isn't about trying to restrict a person's private thoughts, because it's human nature to notice the attractiveness of others; remember, even Jimmy Carter admitted he had lusted after women in his heart. We're talking *behavior* here—behavior that crosses the line of decency and makes someone feel cornered, uncomfortable, or violated.

It all boils down to one word: permission. . . .

Unequal Pay Is a Well-Established Nationwide Problem

Ann Friedman

Ann Friedman writes political and social commentary for The American Prospect Online, The Huffington Post, Mother Jones, Momentum, *and* Feministing.com, *a Web site for feminists that she also edits.*

In the following selection, Friedman explains how after working for twenty years at a Goodyear tire factory in Gadsden, Alabama, Lilly Ledbetter was left an anonymous note showing that she (the only woman on the payroll) had always been paid significantly less than men for the same work. She appealed immediately to the Equal Employment Opportunity Commission. Her case for restitution was eventually overturned by the Supreme Court of the United States. It was not only a loss for Ledbetter, Friedman determines in an interview, but also a blow to thousands of other workers and the Civil Rights Act itself. But in January of 2009, the Senate passed and President Barack Obama signed the Lilly Ledbetter Fair Pay Act into law. It is intended to bring justice to hundreds of women like Ledbetter. The problem can never be completely resolved for Ledbetter, Friedman notes. Because of her decades of lower pay, Ledbetter receives lower retirement and social security payments and has less savings.

Of all the appalling decisions the [John G.] Roberts Court issued last year [2007], one of the worst was the 5–4 ruling in *Ledbetter v. Goodyear*, which gutted the equal-pay provisions of the Civil Rights Act and overturned a decades-old employment-law precedent.

Ann Friedman, "TAP Talks with Lilly Ledbetter," *The American Prospect*, April 23, 2008. Reproduced with permission from *The American Prospect*, 11 Beacon Street, Suite 1120, Boston, MA 02108.

The plaintiff, Lilly Ledbetter, worked for nearly two decades at a Goodyear Tire plant in Gadsden, Alabama. She brought an Equal Employment Opportunity Commission (EEOC) complaint against Goodyear after she discovered that for years she had been paid less than male co-workers with the same job. The justices ruled that employees can only file a wage-discrimination complaint within 180 days of when the payroll decision was made.

After the Supreme Court issued its decision, which leaves women and minorities in Ledbetter's situation with no recourse, congressional Democrats pledged to pass legislation that would give employees two years to file a complaint, in accordance with the law before the Supreme Court issued its decision. The Senate is considering the Lilly Ledbetter Fair Pay Act this week [April 2008], and *TAP* [*The American Prospect*] talked with Ledbetter, who was in Washington to push for the bill's passage.

Ann Friedman: How did you finally find out how much your male co-workers were making?

Lilly Ledbetter: The only way that I really knew was that someone left an anonymous note in my mailbox showing my pay and the pay for the three males who were doing the same job, just on different shifts. Until then, I had no proof. I'd hear people talking about how much they were making when that individual and myself were splitting someone else's shift, and I knew mine wasn't near theirs, but I had no proof. Until I got that scrap of paper. And I went immediately to EEOC.

Did you ever find out who left you the note?

No, I didn't. I'd be afraid to guess. But whoever it is, I'd like to thank them. When I saw the difference in the amount of money I was paid, I could not let Goodyear get away with it. I had to stand up.

How did you know your rights? What led you to sue?

There's a lot of publicity about EEOC and your rights, and I knew I was a lone female in a male-dominated factory. When

I saw that note, it just floored me. I was so shocked at the amount of difference in our pay for doing the same exact job. When we got into the case, I was more shocked to see what all the other people were making, too. They all had much greater pay than I, and most had less seniority, less experience. And I worked there for 20 years. I was a good employee, and I worked hard; there was nothing I couldn't do.

What advice would you give working women when it comes to getting the wages they deserve?

It's a very difficult thing to do anything about. For one thing, if you're one of very few women working in a job, if you rock the boat or ask a question, they say you're a trouble-maker. I'd been in meetings where higher people in my plant would say, "We don't need women in this factory," but they knew the law required them to have some. I sat through those meetings, and I was discriminated against because I did my job and I liked my job, and I was good at it.

Women need to observe, pay attention, be alert. And if possible, have a mentor to help them along the way. If they get any written proof of discrimination, they need to hold onto it. But it's difficult if a corporation goes into it knowing they're going to discriminate.

Is that what was happing at Goodyear?

I don't know. When I first learned, I thought it was just a Southern "good old boy" policy. But I've since learned this is national. It's a civil-rights issue.

What do you say to people who claim that the wage gap is not due to discrimination, it's just that women choose lower-paid work and drop out of the work force to raise children?

No! No, no, no, no. I have had my eyes opened up a great deal being involved in this. I filed my charge in 1998; I've been working with this situation since that time. I have correspondence [from people in similar situations] from all over the United States. I was born and reared in Alabama, and I thought this was just a Southern problem. But it's not—it's a national problem. It doesn't only affect line workers like I was but professional people like doctors and university professors. It's not right, and it's high time for women to be paid equal.

I've had correspondence from women who work two jobs and still can't make ends meet because they aren't paid as well as men. When you carry the responsibility of a job and do your duties, you should be paid and compensated accordingly. I worked for a company that told me, "You do not discuss wages with anyone in this factory." You're very limited when working for a corporation that has those rules, because no one is going to stand around and discuss what they're making.

In my case, the money I should have been compensated hurt me, because my retirement was based on what I earned. So that was much lower. I'm like a second-class citizen for the rest of my life. I will never be compensated for my lower wages and my pension, and Social Security wages are much lower, because Goodyear paid me less. . . . There are a lot of highly qualified women, and they work hard, right alongside those men.

The Supreme Court said I had to have complained within 180 days, within six months of the first paycheck I was given. But I had no way of knowing it was discrimination. My attorney argued it should be based on the paycheck-accrual law. This bill is only going to change the law back to like it was. We've had a lot of opposition that said this would just open up a multitude of lawsuits, and it would be tough on corporations to fight these cases. But that's not true. If a person or individual thinks they have a case, they can't even go to EEOC unless they have proof. You can't just waltz into EEOC.

With equal pay, the law on the books today only allows an individual to go back two years. That's not changing. I had some folks say, "You just waited in the bushes 20 years to collect the big pay day." That's not true! I needed that money when my children were in college, and to feed them and pay the bills. After lawyers' expenses, and taxes on that, any reasonable person can see there wasn't a big bonus there. I've been in this since 1998, and I've been on this road because it's high time that people have a voice and speak up.

The Muslim Woman's Veil Is a Symbol of Faith and Family as Well as of Oppression

Azadeh Moaveni

Azadeh Moaveni is an Iranian American raised in the United States who went to Iran for a few years as a journalist for Time. *She eventually returned to the United States, where she has worked as a journalist and author.*

Moaveni's introduction to Iran, when she returns with her family to the capital city of Tehran, is shocking to her. In the following excerpt, she describes how she finds herself out of place in the armies of rich men's mistresses, whom she encounters in gyms and restaurants. The required veil only deepens and intensifies the Iranian women's characteristic depression—worsened still by smog, unemployment, and "fundamentalist theocracy." The veil and dress (roopoosh) encourage slovenliness and make it difficult to eat. When an Iranian fashion designer regrets her audience's attraction to Western culture, Moaveni wonders if that attraction is actually to Western freedom. Ultimately, even after her return to the United States, Moaveni is torn between the veil's representation of the damaging oppression of Iranian women and the faith and enculturation of loving, male family and friends who support the veil.

Many of the women [at the gym] were obviously the mistresses of these rich men because they were too young, breathtakingly beautiful, and middle class to afford the place otherwise. They carried themselves with a defensive, haughty brazenness that only kept women would think to affect. Oth-

Azadeh Moaveni, "I'm Too Sexy For My Veil," in *Lipstick Jihad: A Memoir of Growing Up Iranian in America and American in Iran*, New York, NY: PublicAffairs, 2005, pp. 149–70. Copyright © 2005 by Azadeh Moaveni. All rights reserved. Reprinted by permission of PublicAffairs, a member of Perseus Books, L.L.C.

ers were simply high-end call girls, a trainer eventually explained to me, when I asked why they were taking photos of each other doing erotic leg lifts on the machines. They exercised with small movements—crossing and uncrossing legs, retouching their makeup, and sipping tea. If they broke a sweat, it was because they had gone up to the roof to tan, or sat in the sauna after a massage, their activity of choice. On those rare occasions they moved quickly enough to actually raise their heart rate, they rushed immediately afterwards to the club café for a reviving, dainty three-course meal.

For some reason, they hated me. Maybe it was because I spurned the cloying ladies' maid/valet, or dashed in and out without the requisite fifteen minutes of languorous small talk. Maybe because I was young, like them, but a non-mistress, unlike them. Perhaps if they knew that I worked, that my life included more pressure than leisure—deadlines and all-nighters, indecent clerics, and a perpetual fearfulness of Mr. X—they would be less resentful. But they clearly believed I rushed home every day to be fed sugar-dusted grapes and fanned with a palm frond, and they tortured me with incessant, niggling assertions of their authority over the world of the gym. It seemed the less power women had in the world outside, the more they sought to flex their influence in the small universe inside. In the non-mistress-run gyms, as I would discover, people pretty much left you alone. But here, each day it was something new: "Ms. Moaveni, can you please put your flip-flops *inside* the cubby holes, and not *next* to them? Can you please change in the dressing room [there was no one around, *ever*, and I used a towel]? Can you place your mobile [phone] on the left of the treadmill rather than to the right?" . . .

The Veil Smothers

The next morning, I drove through the whitish haze of city smog to Qeytariyeh Park. Scores of exercising women filled the park, power-walking laps around the perimeters, their arms pumping vigorously, or splayed out on the lawn, stretching. Though I had put on the lightest cotton veil I owned, I began to swelter, once my body warmed up. There must be something wrong with me, I thought, all these women are doing just fine, what's my problem? Running, I concluded, must raise your body temperature higher than walking, and the head scarf prevents your neck and ears from cooling you down. I tried to stick it out, tried to get to that point where I forgot I was running, absorbed in the smell of the grass, the rhythm of my strides. But the whole time I imagined portly ministers treading water in the Farmanieh pool (the latest thing for the *aghayoon*, the gentlemen, was swimming lessons), and I overheated as much with irritation and resentment. . . .

The women in the room [after a yoga class] rested peacefully, with blissful smiles on their faces. I could not recall ever seeing such a relaxed crowd of Iranian women, who typically began to provoke one another in groups larger than five. The general stressors of Tehran life—toxic smog, traffic jams, fundamentalist theocracy, inflation, unemployment—together with the special burden of the veil made Iranian life particularly wearisome for women, who were depressed in large numbers. The depression had a major, physical component, in that it was compounded by the clothing regulations of the regime.

[Supreme religious and political leader] Ayatollah Khomeini probably did not consider the damage the veil would inflict on women's hair, when he mandated Islamic modesty. Besides split ends and a perpetual lack of volume, the veil intensified the general sadness many women were prone to feeling over all the things that were wrong in their personal lives, and in the country at large.

Why do your hair if it's going to be covered all day? Why watch your figure if it gets lost in the folds of a cloak? And in fact, it really *didn't* make sense to spend half an hour blow-drying your hair only to cover it up. And in the heat, as well as in the cold, it was exponentially more comfortable to wear sweats or leggings or nothing at all underneath the *roopoosh*. As a result, women often found the fine line between a practical approach to Islamic Republic grooming and slovenliness blurred. Before you knew it, you had devolved into a sloppy version of yourself, with unkempt hair (oh, skip a washing day, no one'll see it anyway), alternately clad in mumu-like *roopoosh* outside, and messy house clothes inside. On the occasions when [Aunt] Khaleh Farzi and I tended to our appearances for dinner parties, we would check each other out and exclaim, ahhh! I forgot what you looked like! . . .

Reclaiming Some Integrity Through Fashion

The next morning, as I sat in traffic, I called up everyone in my mobile phone's memory and told them I was on my way to a *fashion show!* Just saying those two words was exhilarating, but mostly no one believed me. There had been no fashion shows in Iran since 1979, when the revolution ordered women to cover themselves, and it was easier for my friends to believe that I was wrong (perhaps I had misread some notice in the paper?) than to imagine such a looming wall could crumble. A security guard stood outside the giant auditorium where the show was to be held, making sure only women entered. A few young men loitered outside, trying to peek inside the door when it swung open.

One part of me shivered with delight at the thought of a fashion show in the Islamic Republic. A public event dedicated to the expression and aesthetic of femininity, in a place so hostile to all things feminine and physical. Another part of me registered disappointment, because a regime-sanctioned catwalk signaled a societal entrenchment of the veil. I'd much rather be driving to a demonstration where women burned head scarves, rather than modeled them. But I reminded myself that women's absorption in their physical appearance, in itself, communicated a powerful message. It meant they were not forfeiting their bodies, their right to express themselves, enshrined in the seemingly superficial but deeply symbolic matter of outer garb.

Excited young women filled the auditorium. I couldn't understand why they didn't remove their veils, since men were not permitted, but the veil had been internalized enough that in many such situations, women needlessly kept them on. The murmur of voices subsided, as the lights dimmed and a remix of Sting's "Desert Rose" came on. The first collection consisted of clothes you could actually wear in public, an impressive array of short coats, tunics, and dresses, cut so they could be worn outdoors as *roopoosh*, but fine enough to be worn indoors as a top. This cleverly solved the problem of having to choose two outfits each day: the *manteau*/outer layer, and the under-layer that you would wear upon arrival at your destination. Inspired, I scribbled in my notebook: Have Arash make knee-length tunic with matching pants, and reversible silk coat.

Next came evening wear. Banal prom gowns, mostly, but a ripple of pleasure passed through the crowd, and they cheered energetically, as though they were imagining themselves making grand appearances at parties in those very outfits. There were only two looks on display, in keeping with the dated ways of being Iranian culture offered women: tart or lady. The lady aesthetic was demure, with lots of tulle and pastel sheaths. The vampy look involved slinky black dresses with lots of sequins. Both were covered in fur coats the models shimmied out of halfway down the runway.

As the models sauntered up and down the catwalk to the deep bass of jungle music, baring nose-rings, navels, and shoulders, something seemed off. Oh, I realized, it was the absence of clicking cameras and flashes going off. There would be no news reports or reviews of this fashion show in the local press. Like it never happened.

The author discusses the effects of the veil on Iranians in Iran and on herself in the United States. Image copyright © Jose AS Reyes, 2009. Used under license from Shutterstock .com.

Alleged Rejection of Western Models

Afterward, I found the designer backstage, and asked her how she had managed to pull off a fashion show. The official sponsor, she said, was a cultural preservation organization that had registered the show as an exhibition of clothes embroidered by traditional handiwork. Then she launched into a lecture on how Iranians needed to create indigenous fashions and that we should "cross out the model of the West as inappropriate." An emaciated model in designer underwear tapped her on the shoulder and asked if she could wear the finale white wedding dress at the afternoon show.

Between the navel rings and the Kate Moss models, I wasn't sure exactly how the West was being rejected. Don't you think young women favor Western fashion because they associate that style with a freer, more open lifestyle? I asked the designer. She blinked disingenuously, as though she could not fathom what I meant.

Iranian women, like women everywhere, expressed themselves in part through their physical appearance. Because the regime tried to take away this right by giving them uniforms, that task became a time-consuming, often obsessive challenge. This was not an overly intellectual or even original point. And it was breathtaking, how people who accommodated, and were accommodated by, the regime (often out of simple opportunism, like this fledgling designer), refused to admit it.

Oh well. Even if she was deluded or a hypocrite, at least she was creating clothes that Iranian women from all walks of life—not just the privileged women of northern Tehran—could feel good about wearing. She showed me the line she had designed for public-sector workers—well-cut tunic-pants combinations, in violets, and olives, with delicate embroidery, as an alternative to the drab smocks they presently wore. Her best uniforms, though, were designed for Iran Air flight attendants, who for twenty years had flown looking like veiled crows. They were a rip-off of the uniforms the stewardesses on Emirates, a Gulf airline wore, but again, I forgave her. There was only so much you could do to jazz up a navy-blue *hijab*. . . .

A Woman's Reason for Leaving

I had always wanted to ask her [my father's cousin Mitra] about why she had decided to leave Iran. . . . Was it hard deciding to go, I asked. You stuck it out for so many years, what made it finally unbearable? She thought about it for several seconds. . . . When she finally did speak, it was not about the veil, or the violations of private life, or any of the daily degradations I had lived and expected to hear about. I couldn't stand arguing with them anymore, she said, the Sister Fatimehs and Sister Zeinabs at the girls' schools.

Mitra had two daughters, both teenagers. They would come home from school, having learned nothing useful, but with an earful of reprimands. "I would go down there every day, and ask them why my daughters were being treated like this. And *they*, these uneducated, unforgiving women, would stare down their noses at me, like, who was I to be asking questions about my daughters' education."

Every life in Iran came with its unique set of battles, most of which, like Mitra's, were unknown to me. I had never tried to raise children under the Islamic Republic, so that particular challenge did not even occur to me. I couldn't imagine what it would be like sending my daughters off to school each day, to be indoctrinated against me, their heads filled with an ideology that I would then need to unteach them at home. To be told that I, their mother, was anti-revolutionary, Westernized, immoral. Had I a choice, I realized, I might not have stayed to fight. Not if it meant sacrificing my daughters. The way I had learned to conceive of the Iranian nation, of devotion to homeland, was, after many months, still abstract. If I had children here, being pried from me and claimed for the revolution, if I had to go through a divorce under a system that stripped me of all my rights, then perhaps these notions of patriotism and loyalty would sound hollow.

Mitra's cheek gently fell against a cushion, and her exhalations became regular. In the quietness of the moment, as twilight settled on the willow trees outside the window, I felt some of the guilt of belonging to the diaspora, to the tribe who left, recede. Through living here, through seeing all the complexity that went into people's decisions to stay or leave, I was learning not to judge so harshly myself or others over such an intensely personal choice.

I respected Mitra for boxing up a privileged life, saying goodbye to all of her extended family, and starting from scratch in another hemisphere. Leaving was not an act of treason or disloyalty but of self-preservation. I had always believed that we outside were compromised for leaving Iran behind. That belief had colored my life, filled it with remorse for a decision that had not been mine. But for Mitra, and thousands of mothers like her, it would have been more compromising *not* to leave. Sacrificing a middle-aged life was one thing. Sacrificing two fresh daughters entirely another. . . .

Imprisoned Behind the Veil

First there was my opposition to the veil, inherited from both sides of my family, an heirloom value that every single one of us—monarchists, secularists, socialists, capitalists, dilettantes—held dear. We did not negotiate with the veil. It was the symbol of how everything had gone horribly wrong. How in the early days of the revolution, secular women wore the veil as a protest symbol against the West and its client state policies, and then had it imposed on them by the fundamentalist mullahs who hijacked the revolution and instituted religious law. My generation, Iranians who learned about 1979 at kitchen tables in the United States, absorbed this version of history as truth. Though most women in modern-day Iran might not consider the veil their highest grievance, they knew it symbolized the system's disregard for women's legal status in general. Mandatory veiling crushed women's ability to express themselves, therefore denying them a basic human right.

As a child of this diaspora, how could I wear the mullahs' veil on the streets of New York? As a student of a liberal American education, taught to apply my political beliefs to my everyday life—to recycle and vote, to respect picket lines and observe boycotts—how could I not take a personal stand against the repressive veil? Did I not owe it to the thousands of Afghani women, veiled by force under the Taliban, the millions of Iranian women who had no choice, to take a stand, when I did? . . .

Veiled, I would dislike myself. I would brush my teeth in the dark, embarrassed to look at myself in the mirror. But going bareheaded, I would display disrespect for the faith of men I esteemed. Men who had, on their territory, encouraged me, treated me with respect, and always helped me, even when it didn't serve their purposes. On what they perceived as my territory, I would be flinging it all in their faces. This I would carry around like a brick of guilt in my stomach. This I could not live with.

Women Slowly Fight Oppression in Saudi Arabia

Basma al-Mutlaq

Basma al-Mutlaq is a professor of statistics in Jordan who received her PhD in feminist literature of the Middle East from London University. She also writes for the Arab News, Brunei Times, *and other journals.*

The presence of so many different groups within Saudi Arabia makes it difficult to establish a women's movement there, reports Basma al-Mutlaq in the following viewpoint. The central group is ruled by ultraconservative Muslims. The fundamental family structure has always been rigidly patriarchal, with fathers, brothers, and husbands dictating women's every move. The government fights against all reforms for women, even maintaining a ban against women driving cars. A few welfare organizations and societies run by upper-class women have privately worked for women of all classes, but change is occurring far too slowly, al-Mutlaq argues. Women who do have the courage to become activists, such as journalist Iman al-Kahtani, are denounced as infidels. Academic women have also been reformers but have been punished by losing their jobs and passports.

When I was asked to talk about the issue of 'sisterhood' in Saudi Arabia I thought it shouldn't be a problem; yet the more I thought about it, the more confused I became. To approach the issue of 'sisterhood' in this part of the world, one has to step aside and view it from different angles: the demographic, political, social, religious and economic.

Basma al-Mutlaq, "Sisterhood in Saudi Arabia," *SaudiAmber: Saudi Women Journal,* July 25, 2007. Reproduced by permission.

Difficulty Establishing Sisterhood

Saudi Arabia's population, as of July 2006, is estimated to be about 27 million. Until the 1960s, most of the population was nomadic or semi-nomadic; due to rapid economic and urban growth, more than 95% of the population now is settled. The issue of 'sisterhood' or at least of a monolithic women's movement in Saudi Arabia is not an easy task; this is due to the heterogeneous nature of the Saudi people—their diverse ideologies and backgrounds. People from the Eastern province are known for their identification and kinship with people in the neighbouring Gulf States. The same principle applies to the people of the Western province, who were educated in, and exposed from an early time to Egypt. Najd, the heart of Saudi Arabia, has long been isolated from any foreign influence and it is the birthplace of the Salafi Wahabis, the political Islamist movement responsible for the ultra conservative interpretation of Islam that dictates the way of life in Saudi Arabia.

To give a more comprehensive overview of the situation of women in Saudi Arabia, we should first look at the patriarchal family structure that is exemplified by submission to the head of the family, who not only maintains a firm grip on women but also manipulates the women's basic decisions in life: career, marriage, as well as other public activities. Bolstered by the Shari'a [Islamic law] and the state law which gives him authority over the female members of the family, the male guardian of the family—be it a father or a brother—can deny his sister, daughter, or mother permission to take a job, travel, open a business . . . etc. Secondly we need to look at the Salafi discourse in Saudi Arabia that is responsible for the political-religious milieu which denounces and obstructs any call for women's emancipation and for reform; in other words it makes the formation of any widespread feminist 'sisterhood' very difficult. The politics of Salafi Wahabism are enforced by the 'Committee for the Promotion of Virtue and Prevention of Vice' whose primary objective is to intimidate and threaten individuals, particularly women, who have been the objects of their fierce and openly aggressive 'policing' methods over the past few decades.

The 'prevention of vice' takes various forms—from insulting the good reputation of women to interrogation and forced signing of a consensus paper saying that 'she won't sin again'. Thus women are effectively voiceless, and for fear of being subjected to this absurd treatment, most avoid any involvement in progressive activities. Worst still, many fear that they would indeed be breaking sacred 'traditions' and straying from the straight and righteous path, the Shari'a, by coming into conflict with a political system that endorses the Salafi ideology in all aspects of their lives.

Saudiness and Sexism

The persistence and normalization of this status quo has meant that narrow, misogynistic and oppressive cultural beliefs have come to represent in many people's eyes an authentic expression of Saudiness. The Saudi people also lack interest in public affairs and in the creation of new ideas that may conflict with this dominant discourse and may compromise their otherwise easy and comfortable lifestyles. Meanwhile 'the majority of women' in Saudi Arabia especially the elite share a 'sisterhood' of beauty and fashion secrets, tips on child rearing and education and interior design.

The ultraconservative milieu and the creation of a law that prohibits the creation of NGOs [nongovernmental organizations] in the country have contrived to suppress the emergence of women's societies, clubs, and unions that might lead to a greater feeling of and belief in 'sisterhood' among Saudi women; such cooperation would definitely result in changes to woman's spiritual, social, and economic reality.

Thus, the Ummah [the Muslim community] has legalized the suppression of women and consequently delayed the creation of women's groups and societies that would have helped create a new public discourse. As a result women in Saudi Arabia continue to play a marginal role in the country; the majority of women are critical of any change and denounce modern women's roles such as the business women, the TV presenter, etc.

Although many commentators claim that things are changing, the pace of change remains slow despite women voicing their demands for reform to the Shari'a and the state's suppressive laws.

Challenging the System

Iman al-Kahtani is an example of a modern woman challenging the enforced silence of women in the kingdom. She is not a typical Saudi woman; at 24, her outspoken journalistic output, especially on women's rights, has gained her much fame and some infamy: 'In our interpretation of Islam, women have no identity,' she wrote angrily in an article for the electronic newspaper *Elaph*. According to Sulaiman al-Hattlan, a columnist for *al-Watan* newspaper, 'If there were five Imans in the kingdom, then we would see some changes.'

Iman's rising public profile has elicited furious reactions. 'People tell me that I am an infidel—they say I am a shame to my tribe,' she says coldly. 'But I say that, in this era of globalization, the tribe really does not count any more. What counts is the individual.' Only occasionally does Iman laugh a deep, reluctant laugh, and her young face is heavy with a weight of experience. Her politics are the product of pure rage. 'Young girls here are so oppressed,' she says. 'They receive this education that means you never think about your rights. But I couldn't accept it. I was always angry about it.'

The religious milieu did, however, give birth to important social welfare organisations throughout the country. Elite members of society, especially princesses, established some of the most effective welfare organisations in operation that reflected a 'sisterhood' of philanthropy and spirituality. Under the umbrella of such organisations women from different social strata assist and volunteer in charitable works. They are an impressively organized cooperative; this can be seen through their regular board meetings and workshops.

These organisations are responsible for supplying many impoverished families with necessities; also, they hold approximately two annual bazaars. Beneficiaries from these bazaars are the poor and disenfranchised of society. I interviewed one active and progressive member of an organisation and asked her about feelings of sisterhood among members; I was surprised to learn of the vicious rivalry amongst them. Despite some members' hard work and creativity they are not given enough credit or recognition.

Beyond these social welfare organisations, pious society women arrange religious meetings at home, forming a strong bond of 'sisterhood' based on spirituality and charity. Through welfare organisations and religious meetings women are helping encourage other women to follow Islamic teachings and source funds for the needy in the kingdom and abroad.

The Price of Resistance

Progressive women, in particular academics, are politically involved and show a strong 'sisterhood' bond that resulted in 1990 in the only organized car demonstration against a proposed official ban on women's driving. They were, however, punished by the religious sects: expelled from their academic posts and their passports [were] confiscated for a year.

The subsequent issuing of an official ban on women's driving was a lesson not only for those who participated in the demonstration but for others who were forced to witness the socially and religiously conservative elements in society railing against their 'decadent' behaviour. This disproportionate punishment had a negative impact on modernists and progressives in Saudi Arabia who knew that their clash was not solely with the system but rather with the religious sects who would turn this basic human rights issue into one of religion and would be quick to besmirch the honour of any woman who dared to challenge them.

Other examples of 'sisterhood' among the educated may be found in private intellectual salons and book clubs in the elite circles of [the cities of] Riyadh and Jeddah; such activities are nevertheless exclusive in nature. They are scheduled and take place in private, as their event is passed on by word of mouth. One should at this point remember the 'prison culture' of the Arab world which thwarts any efforts to create an alternative to the strict political-religious mainstream in these societies.

Asian Women's Careful Rise to Power

Sheridan Prasso

Sheridan Prasso is an author and journalist who has covered Asia extensively. Her specialties are international relations and a variety of global issues.

In the following selection, Prasso interviews Asian women who have struggled and achieved political power in parts of Asia that are notoriously sexist. Some women have achieved power traditionally, through their husbands or fathers, and worked quietly for the cause of women, Prasso observes. Others, such as Reiko Nakajima of Japan, are doubly disadvantaged. Reiko is not only a woman, but also a farmer. She built a political base, ran for office, and won the mayor's seat in her town in 2002. Prasso also discusses two politically powerful women in South Korea who represent opposite views on how best to achieve progress for women. Kang Gaum Sil, the first cabinet minister, believes she could never have reached her position had she not remained feminine (that is, soft-spoken and accommodating). On the other hand, Kim Kang, a police superintendent, believes she would never have reached her position without aggressively fighting for her rights.

Don't turn around," my backseat companion ordered in her posh, Oxford-accented English as we sped through the streets of Rangoon in a white Toyota Corolla. Our pursuers were agents from the five branches of internal security and intelligence of Burma's military regime, she said, and if I showed them my face they would take my picture for the files they kept on people considered dangerous enemies of the state. . . .

Sheridan Prasso, "Power Women," in *The Asian Mystique: Dragon Ladies, Geisha Girls, and Our Fantasies of the Exotic Orient*, New York, NY: PublicAffairs, 2005, pp. 362–86. Copyright © 2005 by Sheridan Prasso. All rights reserved. Reprinted by permission of PublicAffairs a member of Perseus Books, L.L.C.

Some Women Inherit Power

Suu Kyi represents the type of Asian female political leader to have reached global prominence, daughters or wives of former male leaders who inherited the mantle of political power from men. Suu Kyi is the daughter of nationalist hero Aung San, who was assassinated after negotiating independence from colonial ruler Britain in 1947, when Suu Kyi was two years old. Because of this acceptance of women inheriting power, Asians elected the world's *first* female head of government, and they have elected more prominent women leaders than any other region of the world. . . .

One reason for [the] transference of power from husband to wife or father to daughter involves Hindu tradition—which, for the purposes of this discussion, has some influence in the politics of Burma, Indonesia, and other parts of Indianized Southeast Asia. Hindu girls are *paraya dhan*, or "somebody else's wealth." When women marry they take on the caste and status of their husbands—and that can also translate into his political power after his death. . . .

The list of nearly a dozen Asian women inheriting the mantle of power from husbands or fathers includes Corazon Aquino of the Philippines, whose husband Benigno was ordered assassinated by Ferdinand Marcos, and current President Gloria Macapagal Arroyo, who is the daughter of the pre-Marcos Philippine President Diosdado Macapagal. It also includes Megawati Sukarnoputri of Indonesia. Derided by most who meet her as not particularly bright, being the daughter of her late father Sukarno (who ruled Indonesia from 1945 to 1967) was the only qualification she needed for the presidency. Dubbed the "Queen of Silence" by Indonesians who grew dismayed with her inability to rule, however, she was not reelected to a second term in 2004.

Increasingly, however, there is a new kind of woman winning public office in Asia—who through her own education and experience is being valued as a political leader in her own right. In discussions with a dozen female assembly members, mayors, governors, cabinet secretaries, civil service officers, and parliamentarians in Asia, I found that after the wives and daughters of elected men have lowered the barriers to public office, these women without titles or political inheritances are starting to break through them. . . .

From the Ground Up

It would take another entire book to do justice to their stories, to show how so many women have struggled to build their political awareness from the ground up. But one woman who is emblematic of them is Reiko Nakajima, the mayor of Haki, Japan. . . .

"I am forty-eight years old and I am a farmer," she begins. She grows shitake mushrooms, gingko nuts, and rice. Her husband is a civil servant, but he comes from a farming family. When Reiko married him, she moved onto the family farm—with four generations of her husband's family under the same roof. "Walking three steps behind your husband, so to speak, is still prevalent especially in the agricultural areas here. That's why I ran for Mayor." . . .

Reiko worked out in the fields, and started wondering about it all, about the status of women. Perhaps it was time for a change, she thought, so her daughter wouldn't have the same destiny. . . .

So, in 1994, Reiko formed a study group of some women she knew. She invited a few farm women at first, then the owners of the nearby hot spring hotels, who were mostly women. They invited a few shop owners, and they knew some retired women who used to be office workers. Reiko named it the "Ms. Association," and she told the members they were going to "change the landscape" of their lives. Eventually the group swelled to about forty women. . . .

They encouraged Reiko to run for one of twenty-four seats in the town assembly in 1995. No woman had ever run before. "At first my husband and parents were opposed. He said he would divorce me, but he didn't. Many people said, 'No woman can do this job.' But I was so determined. I thought that if I back away from everything I had achieved so far, I would be lost."

The town was shocked when Reiko received 581 votes, the highest number of any candidate in the race. . . .

Reiko ran for Assembly again in 1999 and nearly doubled her votes to 987—again the highest number. The candidate garnering the fewest number of votes to earn a seat got 280. "Many men had said, 'You just got votes because people are curious about you, and you'll lose the second time. So I was elected the second time. But I was still not elected chair of the Assembly. They made me a committee chairperson instead." Reiko then ran for mayor in 2002. She became Mayor Naka-jima, the fifth woman elected mayor in all of Japan's roughly 3,200 municipalities. Now she is the boss of all the stalwart men in the Assembly. Her old Assembly seat was won by an-other woman.

Feminine Toughness

If China had allowed an election to be held in Hong Kong in 1997 instead of hand-picking a man to lead, it most likely would have been won by Anson Chan. She was chief secretary, the top-ranking civil servant and Hong Kong's highest-ranking woman, from 1993 until her resignation in 2001. In other words, she ran the day-to-day operations of the 190,000-employee government, even though Britain had a governor until the 1997 "handover" and China installed a "chief executive" after that. . . .

To fight discrimination, Chan and some colleagues set up a trade union that, through long, slow, persistent struggles, achieved pay parity for women in government service by 1975 and benefits parity by 1982. Benefits amounted to up to 66 percent of take-home pay, so they were worth the continued seven years of fighting. "I've never felt that the best way forward was to take very extreme action, like taking to the streets, burning your bra and whatnot," she said. . . .

I asked her about her public image, about being described from time to time as "Dragon Lady" by the Hong Kong press.

I think, subconsciously, it comes back to this question of stereotypes. You must know that certain attributes in a male are not quite so acceptable in a female. It's spoken of in very disparaging terms, like, if you're being too aggressive. . . .

[As a woman,] everything you do, the way you talk, the way you walk, the way you dress, the way you look, projects either a favorable image of the government or an unfavorable one. So you have a duty. But to achieve equality you don't have to give up your femininity.

Mrs. Chan's assertion is a matter currently being debated by women in power in South Korea. Women are starting to break into public life, despite Korea's reputation as the most conservative, Confucian-influenced culture in Asia—a country where women quit their jobs after marriage with even higher frequency than in Japan. . . .

One of the women breaking the barrier is Kang Gum Sil, the first woman to be appointed to a cabinet minister position in South Korea. She told me that if she hadn't maintained her feminine traits—speaking softly, acting flexibly, and being nice and polite—she never would have reached the level of justice minister (the equivalent of U.S. attorney general).

I later met a prominent feminist and writer in Seoul who was angry with Minister Kang for not acting tough enough and setting a public example for other Korean women on how to fight to get ahead in a man's world. But Minister Kang had told me that it is precisely her refusal to give up her feminine traits that has made her a role model. Schoolgirls write essays about her being their hero, she said. But even more importantly, Minister Kang has been mentioned as a possible future presidential candidate. She is wildly popular. "Maintaining femininity is no longer seen as a disadvantage, but as an advantage," she told me. She was wearing a bright pink linen blazer over a mauve dress, a pink-faced watch with a pink leather band, a pink necklace and matching earrings, and a purple bracelet. . . .

Women in Power

But there are others in Korea who think women need to project toughness instead, to achieve full equality. Fight injustice, stand up for your rights, and challenge the men who are holding you back is what the most senior female police superintendent, Kim Kang Ja, who dressed in all black for our discussion, thinks. If she hadn't done that, she believes, she never would have reached her position. "I have a lot of force in my small body," Superintendent Kim told me when I visited her office at police headquarters in Seoul.

Superintendent Kim said she never takes holidays and works even on Sundays until 10 PM. "Being a police officer fits my character. When I walk down the street and see the insects of our society eating the leaves, I can't just walk past it. I have to do something."

In 1995 Superintendent Kim was denied promotion again, "because I am a mere, meek woman," she said. . . .

But one day [the commissioner] personally came up to me and complimented my work. Because I had worked so hard, the security in my area was spotless. Everything was perfect. After that, people began to think that women could be good at police work, so they put other women into those jobs. Then I was put in charge of three police bureaus, and became the highest ranking police woman in the country. . . .

When I met Korea's most successful businesswoman, Kim Sung Joo, founder and CEO [chief executive officer] of Sung-joo International, she told of [her] struggle [to power].

My first mission was that I just wanted to prove women can do as good a job as men. I wanted to prove women's strength

Indra K. Nooyi, chairman and CEO of PepsiCo, Inc., is one example of an Asian woman who has risen to power in the corporate world. Stan Honda/AFP/Getty Images.

and advance their "soft power." Men use more muscles, a macho way of working. To succeed without drinking, without bribing and without engaging in corruption like that, that became my second mission. . . .

On the Philippine Campaign Trail

Efren Reyes reached out his hand to help pull me up onto the presidential campaign truck packed with movie stars. In the Philippines, Reyes is the equivalent of, say, Harvey Keitel or Willem Dafoe, an actor with an edge and offbeat looks who often plays the bad guy. Sitting on benches on the flat-bed truck are the likes of Robert DeNiro, Bruce Willis, and Clint Eastwood. Even the Philippines' own Brad Pitt is here. It is because one of the most famous movie stars in the Philippines, Fernando Poe, is running for president. And with him on the truck is the "Sweetheart of the Country," his running mate, Loren Legarda. I ask her if she really is a sweetheart.

"No, I'm tough," she answers bluntly. Sometimes a political slogan is *just* a political slogan.

The Philippines loves Loren. She was the youngest woman ever elected to the Senate, at age thirty-eight, and she gained prominence as she rose to Senate Majority Leader in her six years in office. She resigned from the Senate to run for the vice-presidency. The reason she was running with Poe instead of being invited onto the ticket of incumbent President Gloria Arroyo, she said, is because then there would be a double-woman slate running for the highest elected offices in the country.

The percentage of women holding elected office in the Philippines is high compared to that of the rest of Asia—and even higher than in the United States. Of the Philippine Congress, 17.2 percent are women (of the U.S. Congress, 13.6 percent are women); of seventy-four provincial governors in the Philippines, fourteen are women (18.9 percent); in the United States there were six women out of fifty governors in 2004, and only fifteen women had ever been elected to the office since 1925. But that doesn't mean it's easy. "It's still difficult to be a woman politician in the Philippines," Loren tells me. "You cannot expect fair treatment all the time. Men expect that you are the weaker sex."

Our truck, one of several in a campaign caravan, starts on a long, three-hour journey through the blazing sun. . . .

Our next stop is a country club with a luscious golf course. Loren jumps out of the car and greets the men standing there. "How am I doing in your district?" she asks. It is the provincial vice governor and his brother, a congressman. Their father has spent many years as governor. This is the Remulla family, the power brokers who control Cavite Province on the southern shores of Manila Bay, and this is an important meeting. Loren is seeking their endorsement. It is worth 1.2 million votes.

The Remullas provide a club townhouse for us to freshen up and invite us for dinner in an hour. "Males have a tendency to look at women like me, young, as new kid on the block. But the advantage of being a woman is that you can achieve what men cannot, through your charm," Loren tells me. Later, when I watch her work her magic on the patriarch and his powerful sons at dinner, I see what she means. In the townhouse as we relax in the meantime, Loren takes a shower and puts on a clean version of her jeans-and-white-shirt outfit. Her chief of staff turns on the TV. By coincidence, one of Loren's campaign commercials is on. It features a ten-year-old girl. "When I grow up, I want to be intelligent," she says. Then a scene flashes of Loren shaking hands and picking up babies. "I want to be able to answer all the questions," the girl says. There are more scenes of Loren glad-handing. It concludes with the girl again: "I wish I could vote." Loren's policies have aimed at women's rights, and in the Senate she sponsored anti-domestic violence bills, agricultural projects for women, and anti-trafficking laws. While the commercial is not directly about empowerment, the subliminal message of appealing to women is there.

For Further Discussion

1. In what specific ways does gender isolate and marginalize the women of Mango Street? How, from your own observations, would you compare their situations with that of women in the United States today? (See Bolaki, Bellas, Quintana, McCracken, Guilbault.)

2. The word "house" in Cisneros's work has multiple meanings. Discuss these as both limitations of and liberation from patriarchy. (See Quintana and Doyle.)

3. Compare any male coming-of-age story with that of Esperanza. Consider the similarities as well as the differences in their interests, values, viewpoints, and relationships. (See Gutiérrez-Jones.)

4. Compare a non-Hispanic American female coming-of-age story with that of Esperanza. Consider the similaritites as well as the differences in the kinds of role models to be followed. Are there polar opposite role models? (See Petty.)

For Further Reading

Rudolpho Anaya, *Bless Me Ultima*. New York: Warner Books, 1999.

Mariana Ba, *So Long a Letter*. London: Heinemann, 1981.

Sandra Cisneros, *Loose Woman*. New York: Knopf, 1994.

———, *My Wicked, Wicked Ways*. New York: Knopf, 1992.

———, *Woman Hollering Creek*. New York: Random House, 1991.

Judith Ortiz Cofer, *The Meaning of Consuelo*. New York: Farrar, Strauss, and Giroux, 2003.

Maxine Hong Kingston, *The Woman Warrior*. South Yarmouth, MA: J. Curley, 1978.

Toni Morrison, *The Bluest Eye*. New York: Washington Square Press, 1972.

Amy Tan, *The Joy Luck Club*. New York: Putnam, 1989.

Alice Walker, *The Color Purple*. New York: Pocket Books, 1985.

Bibliography

Books

Rudolfo Anaya   *Aztlan*. Albuquerque: University of New Mexico Press, 1991.

Gloria Anzaldúa, ed.   *Making Face, Making Soul/Haciendo Caras: Creative and Critical Perspectives by Feminists of Color*. San Francisco: Aunt Lute Foundation Books, 1990.

Hector Calderon   *Narratives of Greater Mexico*. Austin: University of Texas Press, 2004.

Susan Faludi   *Backlash: The Undeclared War Against American Women*. New York: Crown, 1991.

Betty Friedan   *The Feminine Mystique*. New York: Norton, 1974.

Angela R. Gillem and Cathy Thompson, eds.   *Biracial Women in Therapy: Between the Rock of Gender and the Hard Place of Race*. Binghamton, NY: Haworth Press, 2004.

Feroza Jussawalla and Reed Way Dasenbrook   *Interviews with Writers of the Post-Colonial World*. Jackson: University Press of Mississippi, 1992.

Ellen McCracken   *New Latina Narrative. The Feminine Space of Postmodern Ethnicity*. Tucson: University of Arizona Press, 1999.

Tey Diana Rebolledo	*Women Singing in the Snow.* Tucson: University of Arizona Press, 1995.
Anna Marie Sandoval	*Toward a Latina Feminism of the Americas: Repression and Resistance in Chicana and Mexicana Literature.* Austin: University of Texas Press, 2009.
Ilan Stavans	*The Hispanic Condition: Reflections on Culture and Identity in America.* New York: HarperCollins, 1995.
Autumn Stephens, ed.	*Roar Softly and Carry a Great Lipstick.* San Francisco: Inner Ocean, 2004.
Jack Zipes, ed.	*Don't Bet on the Prince: Contemporary Feminist Fairy Tales in North America and England.* New York: Methuen, 1986.

Periodicals

Felicia Cruz	"On the 'Simplicity' of Sandra Cisneros's *The House on Mango Street,*" *Modern Fiction Studies,* Winter 2001.
Christina Rose Dubb	"Adolescent Journeys: Finding Female Authority in *The Rain Catchers* and *The House on Mango Street,*" *Children's Literature in Education,* September 2007.
Nazila Fathi	"Starting at Home, Iran's Women Fight for Rights," *New York Times,* February 13, 2009.

Gordon B. Forbes
et al.
"Perceptions of Married Women and Married Men with Hyphenated Surnames," *Sex Roles*, March 2002.

Kate Jeffreys
"Why Women Are Still Oppressed," *Socialist Alternative*, February 2007.

Deborah King
"Patriarchy Is Alive and Well," *Psychology Today: Mining the Headlines*, May 6, 2009.

Dianne Klein
"Coming of Age in Novels by Rudolfo Anaya and Sandra Cisneros," *English Journal*, September 1992.

Philip Longman
"The Return of Patriarchy," *Foreign Policy*, March/April 2006.

Mary Jo Patterson
"Gender Scholar Studies Hyphenation as a Cultural Practice," *Rutgers*, May 27, 2009.

Jonna Lian
Pearson
"Multicultural Feminism and Sisterhood Among Women of Color in Social Change Dialogue," *Howard Journal of Communications*, January 2007.

Katha Pollitt
"Muslim Women's Rights, Continued," *Nation*, June 24, 2009.

Diane-Michele
Prindeville
"Identity and the Politics of American Indian and Hispanic Women Leaders," *Gender & Society*, vol. 17, no. 4, 2003.

Gerald Torres
and Katie Pace

"Understanding Patriarchy as an
Expression of Whiteness: Insights
from the Chicana Movement,"
*Washington University Journal of Law
and Policy*, November 2, 2005.

Index